Dr. Maurice Friedman, who received his Ph.D. in the History of Culture from the University of Chicago, is Professor of Religious Studies, Philosophy and Comparative Literature at San Diego State University. In addition to having written sixteen books, five of them on Buber, one of which (Martin Buber's Life and Work: The Later Years) won the National Jewish Book Award for Biography in 1985, he has translated, edited and introduced a dozen of Buber's works, has contributed chapters to more than fifty books and has published almost 200 articles. A previous book, *Martin Buber and the Eternal*, is also available from Human Sciences Press.

A Dialogue with
Hasidic Tales

A Dialogue with Hasidic Tales

Hallowing the Everyday

Maurice Friedman, Ph.D.

San Diego State University
San Diego, CA

INSIGHT BOOKS

Human Sciences Press
72 Fifth Avenue
New York, NY 10011

BM
532
.F76
1988

Printed in the United States of America
987654321

Library of Congress Cataloging-in-Publication Data

Friedman, Maurice S.
    A dialogue with Hasidic tales.

    Bibliography: p.
    Includes index.
    1. Hasidim—Legends—Meditations.   2. Parables,
Hasidic—Meditations.   I. Title.
BM532.F76   1988   296.8'33   87-22824
ISBN 0-89885-407-5

Contents

For
Aleene Friedman,
Laurel Mannen,
Susan Richards,
and the Hasidic Tale-ers

Acknowledgments

I should like to acknowledge with gratitude permission of Random House and Pantheon Books to reprint passages from Martin Buber, *Tales of the Hasidim: The Early Masters* and *Tales of the Hlasidim: The Later Masters,* both translated by Greta Hort and copyright 1947, 1975 by Schocken Books, New York; from Martin Buber, *Hasidism and Modern Man,* edited and translated with an Introduction by Maurice Friedman, copyright by Horizon Press, 1958; from Martin Buber, *The Origin and Meaning of Hasidism,* edited and translated with an Introduction by Maurice Friedman, copyright by Horizon Press, 1960; and to the Holocaust Publications for permission to reprint passages from *Against Silence: The Voice and Vision of Elie Wiesel,* selected and edited by Irving Abrahamson, copyright 1985 by Irving Abrahamson, published by Holocaust Library, New York.

Preface

This book is not a study of Hasidism or even of Buber's *Tales of the Hasidim*. It is the record and product of almost 40 years of *dialogue* with the Hasidic tales in the form which Buber has given them. Abraham Joshua Heschel once remarked to me: "Everyone has something that he brings as a touchstone. With you it is Hasidism." He was right, but more than "Hasidism," which exists only as an abstraction from the actual life and teachings of the Hasidim, it is the tales of the Hasidim. They have become interwoven with my life in such a way that they have become an integral part of my living and my thinking. As a result, this dialogue has taken place ultimately not for the sake of understanding Hasidism, Martin Buber, or even the tales in themselves, but for the sake of what they have to say to me and my contemporaries about some of the perplexing problems that confront us in everyday life.

This is the spirit in which we have carried on our monthly discussions of these tales for the last 10 years, and it is the spirit of some 20 years of teaching the tales and facilitating "basic encounter group" discussion of the tales that preceded it. For this reason, these groups have seemed to me a significant alternative to academic discussion, with its emphasis on detached intellectual objectivity, on the one hand, and the sensitivity awareness and ordinary encounter groups, with their emphasis upon subjective feeling, on the other. The "basic encounter-discussion group" is one in which the members are called forth in such a way that they respond from the depths without making that response their conscious goal. One person brings in a tale that has spoken to his condition, reads it, discusses his relationship to it, and then the rest of the group enters in, with the story always present to return to as a center and ground. In contrast to the discussion of abstract concepts, in which people pass each other by without knowing it, the Hasidic tale gives a concrete check that helps the participants know where they stand in relationship to the story and to one another.

Two concrete illustrations stay with me from the experience which I had leading discussions of Hasidic tales at Pendle Hill, the Quaker Center for Study in Wallingford, Pennsylvania:

An English Quaker who made a great point of the fact that he was a humble member of the working class once read a story to the group about a man who refused to establish a congregation of his own, even though the Baal Shem twice insisted on it and threatened him with the loss of his share in the world to come. In the original tale, the man's reply was, "I will not do anything that does not befit me." But the English worker read it aloud, "I will not do anything that does not benefit me." No one in the group picked this up except myself, and I did not comment on it. We continued the discussion for a while, and then I asked him to read the tale again. This time every single person in the group caught his substitution simultaneously, and he himself said, "Maybe that says something about me!"

Once at Pendle Hill I counseled a young man whose life was going in a circle and getting nowhere. He had been a theologian, an English major, a pianist; he had taught in Africa; he had almost entered a monastery; he had a wife and child and was on the verge of leaving them. In the group he read a Hasidic tale about "True Sorrow and True Joy," which says of joy:

> He who is devoid of inner substance and, in the midst of his empty pleasures, does not feel it, not tries to fill his lack, is a fool. But

he who is truly joyful is like a man whose house has burned down, who feels his need deep in his soul and begins to build anew. Over every stone that is laid, his heart rejoices.[1]

I was familiar with that tale, but it had never struck me. Now, knowing this man as I did, it moved me a great deal. Ever since, I cannot read or hear it without its evoking that same poignant feeling created in me by his situation at that time. His reading that tale to the group and discussing it with them was, I suspect, the turning point when his life began to become a meaningful way. He too recognized that his house had burnt down, and he had to build it back brick by brick.

I have always vastly preferred Martin Buber's method of grouping the tales together according to the zaddik, or Hasidic rebbe, about whom they are told, to Rabbi Louis Newman's *Hasidic Anthology* in which the tales are grouped according to subject matter, e.g., ethics and the like. The former preserves the uniqueness of the zaddik and of the event; the latter loses them in abstractions. If I must violate Buber's method here for the sake of the topics of each chapter, I do so while preserving the name and usually something of the personal uniqueness and unique approach of the rebbe in whose name the tale is cited. This is consistent with my own claim in my book *Touchstones of Reality* that touchstones are life events that yield insights and attitudes the limits of which are discovered and tested in our new life encounters. From this standpoint, a Hasidic tale may be understood as an embodied event or "touchstone of reality," one that enters into our own dialogue of touchstones and that through that dialogue may become touchstones for us as well.

If our way is a true way, it has to be unique, and if it is unique, it cannot serve as a model. Yet we help one another along the road when we share our touchstones *and* the confusion that sometimes accompanies them. We evolve our touchstones in relation with one another; we witness to one another. We have an impact on one another through which we grow in our own touchstones. Growing in this way, we come to recognize that a "dialogue of touchstones" is itself a touchstone.[2]

It is for these reasons that I, a philosopher and a practicing therapist, choose to communicate with you the reader via the Hasidic tales even at the risk of putting off those of you who are not familiar with them. Many, perhaps most people in America, are not familiar with Hasidism, and many of those who are, are familiar with closed, isolated cults—"communities of affinity, or like-mindedness"—rather than with the open-spirited groups that added such incomparable breadth and depth to the narrow and confined world of rabbinic legalism and ghetto existence in eighteenth- and nineteenth-century Eastern European Jewry.

I do not use the tale as illustration of philosophical abstraction and psychological insight but as the springboard from which both philosophical and psychological understanding arises. It has become quite natural over the years for a Hasidic tale to come to my mind unbidden as I lecture and even as I talk; for these tales are old friends, and many of them are appropriate in more than one context. I was not surprised, therefore, when I read through the first draft of this book to discover that in many cases I had used the same tale in more than one chapter. In most cases I have eliminated this repetition by choosing to leave the tale only in one of the two or three contexts in which it was embedded. In a dozen or so cases, however, I have chosen to leave the repetition because it seemed justified by what was gained through doing so. Usually, I have indicated that this is a tale that we have seen before. Actually, to rediscover a tale in a new aspect is often as much fun as to discover it in the first place!

My greatest indebtedness for this book is obviously to Martin Buber himself, who spent a lifetime learning the proper faithfulness and the proper freedom in selecting and editing these Hasidic tales, or "legendary anecdotes," as he called them. I cannot accept the dismissal implicit in the statement that is occasionally made that in his Hasidic tales, Buber "spoke as an outsider to outsiders." It is true that Buber did not speak only to Hasidic Jews or only to Jews of any sort, but to the Western world to which he brought Hasidism "against its will" because of the need of the hour for an image of authentic personal and social existence. It is true also, as Ernst Simon has pointed out, that Buber did not stress that observance of *halakhah*, or the Jewish law, that was an integral to the original Hasidism as it is to the Lubavitcher or Satmar Hasid of today. But he left nothing of it out, and what he did bring was not, as even Gershom Scholem would agree, a reading into the tales of his own existentialist philosophy but a faithful retelling that will stand the test of time.

My second indebtedness is to my former wife Eugenia Friedman, who for many years co-taught Hasidic tales with me at Pendle Hill, who has shared my love of these tales for more than 30 years now, and who read an early draft of this present book and made some helpful criticisms and suggestions. I am especially indebted, thirdly, to my friend Virginia Shabatay, who labored with me over this manuscript over several months and had the patience and interest to return again to some of the questions that mutually concerned us. Finally, I wish to express my gratitude to Kendra Crossen, Associate Editor of Shambhala Publications, who urged me to focus the book on hallowing the everyday and thus helped me discover its present and, I believe, true form.

Maurice Friedman
Solana Beach, CA
January 1987

PART I

Hasidism and Hasidic Tales

1

Hasidism

Hasidism is the popular mystical movement of East European
Jewry in the eighteenth and nineteenth centuries. The Hebrew
word *hasid* means "pious." It is derived from the noun *hased,*
meaning loving-kindness, mercy, or grace. The Hasidic movement
arose in Poland in the eighteenth century, and, despite bitter per-
secution at the hands of traditional rabbinism, spread rapidly
among the Jews of Eastern Europe until it included almost half
of them in its ranks. Hasidism is really a continuation in many
senses of biblical and rabbinical Judaism. While it is not an historical continuation of Christianity, many people have been startled by the resemblances between Hasidism and early Christianity,
in particular between the founder of Hasidism—the Baal Shem
Tov, or Good Master of the Name of God—and Jesus. Both spoke
to the common, the ordinary folk; both represented something of
a revolt against the overemphasis on learning; both tried to renew
the spirit from within the tradition rather than destroying, cutting
off, and radically changing the tradition.

The Hasidim founded real communities, each with its own
rebbe. The rebbe, the leader of the community, was also called
the zaddik, the righteous or justified person. "The world stands

because of the zaddik," says the Talmud, and in Jewish legend this has grown into the myth of the 36 hidden zaddikim of each generation—the *lamedvovnikim*—without whom the world could not stand. Each one of these zaddikim had his own unique teaching that he gave to his community. Originally as it was passed down from generation to generation, the leadership devolved not so much on those who could receive a doctrine but on those who could embody a way of life. Thus the first effect of the zaddik was to bring the people to immediacy in relationship to God. Later, when hereditary dynasties of Hasidim arose and the rebbes lived in great palaces and were surrounded by awe and superstition, the zaddik became almost a mediator between the people and God—the very opposite of his original function.

Hasidism grew out of the most abstruse speculation—first the medieval kabbala of the Zohar ("The Book of Splendor") and later the Lurian kabbala that arose after the Jews were exiled from Spain in 1492. If you go today to Israel and go up the mountains opposite the Sea of Galilee, winding round and round, you finally reach, near the top, Tzfat, or Safed, where the Lurian kabbala arose. There men strove to bring the Messiah down. At one point in 1544 they all stood on the rooftops expecting that at that hour the Messiah would come. There developed in the Lurian kabbala a marvelous Gnostic doctrine in which the primordial fall was not, as in the Zohar, a gradual emanation of 10 *Sephiroth*. It was instead an event, a happening, in which heavenly vessels were so full of grace that they burst and the sparks of divine light fell downward to earth and were surrounded by shells of darkness. The *tikkun*, or restoration, accordingly meant freeing these sparks from their shells so that they could rise upward to their divine source. This could be done through *kavanot*—mystical intentions with which one prayed and acted. It was believed that one could help bring the Messiah down through the part in the restoration that one's *kavanot* made possible. This led to the pseudo-messianic movement of Sabbatai Zvi, which ended disastrously when Sabbatai Zvi was forcibly converted to Islam. Out of all this ferment and the Chmielnieski Cossack massacres of hundreds of thousands of Jews in village after village in Eastern Europe was kindled the movement founded by Israel ben Eliezer (1700–1760), the Baal Shem Tov, or Good Master of the Name of God. The Baal Shem said, "I have come to teach you a new way, and it is not fasting and penance but joy in God, in Israel, and in the Torah."

Hasidism is a mysticism which does not hold chastity to be the highest virtue. On the contrary, it sees marriage as the highest form of life. It is a mysticism which does not turn away from community, or put aside the life of the senses. Community is to be hallowed, the life of the senses celebrated and sanctified. Hasidism supplemented *kavanot* with *kavana:* it stressed the consecration and direction of the whole person as well as special mystical techniques.

The first Hasidic book that I read was an early attempt at the translation of *The Legend of the Baal-Shem*. This was the first Jewish book that had had any impact on me since I was a child, the first that spoke to me as a mature, thinking man. As I look back on this impact, it was that of the Baal Shem Tov as an image of the human—an image of the *Jew* but also an image of the human that superseded—without displacing—Saint Francis, the Buddha, Sri Ramakrishna, and Jesus in my allegiance. This image was, to be sure, a romanticized one in Buber's highly poetic retelling. Yet it was essentially the same man who spoke to me through these legends as later spoke to me through *The Tales of the Hasidim,* "The Baal Shem Tov's Instruction in Intercourse with God," and the accounts of the life and teaching of the Baal Shem to which I had access through English and German sources. This was the man who pointed out that Isaac and Jacob had to find their own unique relationship to God and could not base their searching on that of Abraham alone, the man who knew his relationship to God as the meaning and goal of his strivings compared to which no future life was of importance. The Besht did not emphasize mystical exercises, such as I had been concerned with, but wholehearted turning to God. He preferred a passionate opponent to a lukewarm adherent. "For the passionate opponent may come over and bring all his passion with him. But from a lukewarm adherent there is nothing more to be hoped." He turned away from asceticism and mortification of the flesh to the joyful recognition that each man is a son of the King. But he did not mistake the son for the King. His last words were, "Let not the foot of pride come near me!"

In Hasidism I found an image of an active love and fervent

devotion no longer coupled with self-denial or metaphysical theo-
rizing about unity with the divine. After my immersion in the in-
dividualistic and world-denying forms of mysticism that I had
found in Hinduism, Buddhism, and Christianity, Hasidism spoke
to me in compelling accents of a wholehearted service of God that
did not mean turning away from my fellowmen and from the world.
All that was asked was to do everything one did with one's whole
strength—not the denial of self and the extirpation of the passions
but the fulfillment of self and the direction of passion in a communal mysticism of humility, love, prayer, and joy. After my concern for techniques of spiritual perfection, I now learned that fulfillment and redemption do "not take place through formulae or
through any kind of prescribed and special action," but through
the *kavana* that one brings to one's every act. "It is not the matter
of the action, but only its dedication that is decisive." A new
image of the human offered itself to me, that of the zaddik—the
humble person, the loving person, the helper:

> Mixing with all and untouched by all, devoted to the multitude
> and collected in his uniqueness, fulfilling on the rocky summits of
> solitude the bond with the infinite and in the valley of life the bond
> with the earthly. . . . He knows that all is in God and greets His
> messengers as trusted friends.[1]

In the end, the most important heritage that Hasidism has
bequeathed us is not its doctrine and teachings but its image of
the human—the image of the Besht, the Maggid of Mezritch, Levi
Yitzhak of Berditchev, Nachman of Bratzlav, Shneur Zalman of
Ladi, the "Yehudi" of Pzhysha, and a host of other zaddikim,
each with a unique relationship to God and to his particular community.

We stand in a stream of general culture which presents us
other, more "spiritual" and less "anthropomorphic" forms of religion than Judaism. After a lecture that I gave on Hasidism to a
Jewish audience, I was astonished at the complaint that Hasidism
was "mechanistic" and had no room for "love." When I had
translated "mechanistic" into "materialistic" in my own mind,
I understood through that "inclusion," or "imagining the real"
that enables us to experience the other side of the relationship,

even with those who are quite other than we are, that the woman who had asked the question was approaching Hasidism from the very un-Jewish but all too familiar dualism between the spiritual and the material, according to which the concern with the everyday automatically signals the exclusion of the truly "spiritual." This widespread and insidious dualism recurs on a higher level in a statement by the Jew Mishe Gordon in *Dr. Zhivago,* the famous novel of the Russian-Jewish poet Boris Pasternak. Speaking of the rejection of Christianity by the Jews, Gordon says: "This glorious holiday from mediocrity, from the dreary, boring constriction of everyday life was first achieved on their soil, proclaimed in their language, belonged to their race! And they actually saw and heard it and let it go!"[2] In Hasidism, Judaism has produced a mysticism that "restores to the element of earth those whom preoccupation with thought had removed from it," while raising "to the heights of heaven . . . those who are burdened with the weight of earth."[3] This knowledge could effect a decisive change in the attitude of those Jewish "seekers" who unconsciously share in the general depreciation of Judaism in Western culture as an inferior form of religion lacking in spirituality.

2

To Tell a Story

When Hermann Hesse nominated Martin Buber for the Nobel Prize in Literature in 1949, it was to Buber's *Tales of the Hasidim* in particular that he pointed in his explanation to a friend: "Martin Buber . . . has enriched world literature with a genuine treasure as has no other living author—*The Tales of the Hasidim*." In his contribution to *The Philosophy of Martin Buber,* Walter Kaufmann said of Buber's *Tales of the Hasidim* that they are definitive in their simplicity, "diamonds" which Buber cut to perfection:

> What saves Buber's work is its perfection. He has given us one of the great religious books of all time, a work that invites comparison with the great Scriptures of mankind. . . . The rank of these works does not depend on their positivistic accuracy but on their profundity, as is true also of *The Tales of The Hasidim.*[1]

This collection grew out of Buber's own long dialogue with a tradition, Kaufmann pointed out, and it loses none of its original impressiveness after one has lived with it for a generation. "These stories will surely be remembered widely when the theologians of our time have gone the way of Harnack and Schleiermacher."

In the title essay of *Hasidism and Modern Man,* Buber narrated how he reached the valid form of the "legendary anecdote" after 40 years of wrestling with the task of retelling "the crude and shapeless traditional material." These legendary anecdotes report the overwhelming reality of the lives of a great series of leaders of Hasidic communities–not in connected biography but in a tremendous series of limited events. Dumb happening and saying alike spoke, not didactically, with any moral attached, but as live events. The task of Buber, the reteller, was to reconstruct the pure event out of the crude formlessness so that the Hasidic life might become visible as reality and teaching. "Even where I had to let theory speak, I could relate it back to the life"—a life which Buber characterized as capable in an especial manner of working on people even today when the spirit in the form of ideas, ideals, and culture no longer has a binding force on everyday life. "Thus grew the form of the legendary anecdote."

> They are called anecdotes because each one of them communicates an event complete in itself, and legendary because at the base of them lies the stammering of inspired witnesses who witnessed to what befell them, to what they comprehended as well as to what was incomprehensible to them; for the legitimately inspired has an honest memory that can nonetheless outstrip all imagination.[2]

Even this does not capture the full significance of the Hasidic tale. In his chapter on Hasidism in *Major Trends in Jewish Mysticism,* Gershom Scholem pointed out that if the zaddik, the leader of the Hasidic community, becomes the center of the new myth, the Hasidic tale about the zaddik is the religious carrying forward of that myth:

> The revival of a new mythology in the world of Hasidism to which attention has been drawn occasionally, especially by Martin Buber, draws not the least part of its strength from its connection between the magical and the mystical faculties of its heroes. When all is said and done it is this myth which represents the greatest creative expression of Hasidism. In the place of the theoretical disquisition, or at least side by side with it, you get the Hasidic tale. Around the lives of the great zaddikim, the bearers of that irrational something which their mode of life expressed, legends

were spun often in their own lifetime. . . . To tell a story of the deeds of the saints has become a new religious value, and there is something of the celebration of a religious rite about it. Not a few great zaddikim . . . have laid down the whole treasure of their ideas in such tales. Their Torah took the form of an inexhaustible fountain of story-telling. Nothing at all has remained theory, everything has become a story.[3]

These reflections take on added depth if we add to them Scholem's statement, "Within a geographically small area and also within a surprisingly short period, the ghetto gave birth to a whole galaxy of saint-mystics, each of them a startling individuality." What is more, as Scholem stressed, this burst of mystical energy did not produce new religious ideas or theories of mystical knowledge but rather "the spontaneity of feeling generated in sensitive minds by the encounter with the living incarnations of mysticism."

Why was the telling of a tale about a zaddik so integrally important to the life of the Hasidim? The answer must surely lie in their recognition that such tale-telling represented a genuine continuation of the life of the zaddik in question, more even, a re-presentation, a making present anew of the religious reality embodied in that life. From this standpoint the telling of a Hasidic tale was never the mere reflection of the past, but a fully present, multidimensional lived event in itself. That this was so is shown by numerous of the Hasidic tales themselves. The second paragraph of Martin Buber's Preface to his *Tales of the Hasidism* is devoted to just such a story:

> A rabbi, whose grandfather had been a disciple of the Baal Shem, was asked to tell a story. "A story," he said, "must be told in such a way that it constitutes help in itself." And he told: "My grandfather was lame. Once they asked him to tell a story about his teacher. And he related how the holy Baal Shem used to hop and dance while he prayed. My grandfather rose as he spoke, and he was so swept away by his story that he himself began to hop and dance to show how the master had done. From that hour on he was cured of his lameness. That's the way to tell a story!"[4]

One of the longest stories that Buber himself includes in the stories about the Baal Shem, the founder of Hasidism, is entitled

The Storyteller. It portrays the Baal Shem telling stories so compellingly that all the congregation of his adversary Rabbi Jacob Joseph, later rav of Polnoye, are detained from attending the morning services. When Jacob Joseph angrily confronts the Baal Shem, the storyteller tells him still another story and wins him over. In Buber's version of the famous story of "Generations" that we also know from Scholem and from Elie Wiesel (who adds: "God made man because He loves stories"), what had earlier been accomplished by prayer and secret *kavanot* (mystical intentions) is now accomplished just by telling the story of these accomplishments:

> The rabbi of Rizhyn related:
> "Once when the holy Baal Shem Tov wanted to save the life of a sick boy he was very much attached to, he ordered a candle made of pure wax, carried it to the woods, fastened it to a tree and lit it. Then he pronounced a long prayer. The candle burned all night. When morning came, the boy was well.
> "When my grandfather, the Great Maggid, who was the holy Baal Shem's disciple, wanted to work a like cure, he no longer knew the secret meaning of the words on which he had to concentrate. He did as his master had done and called on his name. And his efforts met with success.
> "When Rabbi Moshe Leib, the disciple of the disciple of the Great Maggid, wanted to work a cure of this kind, he said: 'We no longer have the power even to do what was done. But I shall relate the story of how it was done, and God will help.' And his efforts met with success."[5]

A closely similar story within a story is told in the name of Rabbi Yitzhak Eisik of Kalev:

> The tale is told:
> The Rabbi of Kalev once spent the Sabbath in a nearby village as the guest of one of the hasidim. When the hour to receive the Sabbath had come, someone suddenly screamed, and a servant rushed in and cried that the barn in which the grain was stored was on fire. The owner wanted to run out, but the rabbi took him by the hand. "Stay!" he said. "I am going to tell you a story." The Hasid stayed.
> "When our master Rabbi Zusya was young," said the zaddik,

"he stoked the stoves in the house of the Great Maggid, for this duty was always assigned to the youngest disciples. Once when he was saying the Psalms with great fervor just before the coming of the Sabbath, he was startled by screams from within the house. Sparks had fallen from the stove which he had filled with wood, and since no one was in the living room, a fire had started.

" 'Zusya!' he was reproached. 'There's a fire!'

" 'No matter,' he replied. 'Is it not written: And the fire abated!' At that very same moment the fire abated."

The rabbi of Kalev fell silent. The Hasid, whom he still held by the hand, did not dare move. A moment passed and someone called in at the window that the fire in the barn had gone out.[6]

Rabbi Menahem Mendel of Kotzk, the famous Kotzker rebbe, said he became a Hasid because in the town where he lived there was an old man who told stories about zaddikim. "He told what he knew, and I heard what I needed." But what about those of us who do not live in such towns or, even if we have access to the tales through the renditions of Buber, Elie Wiesel, and others, live in a time where such continuity with a past where the sacred permeated everyday life now seems unthinkable? For them, or rather for us, since we are all, including myself, in just this situation, there is a tale of one of the later masters that "speaks to our condition," to use the Quaker phrase that so often comes to me in connection with these tales:

One evening several of Rabbi Hayyim of Kosov's Hasidim sat together in his House of Study and told one another stories about zaddikim, above all about the Baal Shem Tov. And because the telling and the listening were very sweet to them, they were at it even after midnight. Then one of them told still another story about the Baal Shem Tov. When he had ended, another sighed from the bottom of his heart. "Alas!" said he, half to himself. "Where could we find such a man today?"

At that instant, they heard steps coming down the wooden stair which led from the zaddik's room. The door opened and Rabbi Hayyim appeared on the threshold, in the short jacket he usually wore in the evening. "Fool," he said softly, "he is present in every generation, he, the Baal Shem Tov, only that in those days he was manifest while now he is hidden."

He closed the door and went back up the stair. The hasidim sat together in silence.[7]

The question was not, "Where could we find another founder of Hasidism today," but "Where could we find such a *man* today?" The answer of Rabbi Hayyim, similarly, was not the comforting knowledge of Isaiah's Immanuel, that God is with us, but that in every age "such a man" exists. In the eighteenth century this man was manifest in the Baal Shem Tov while today he is hidden.

In my book *The Human Way: A Dialogical Approach to Religion and Human Experience,* I speak of "theology as event"—the way that we walk in the concrete situations of our existence. To speak thus means an inversion of traditional theology, which rests upon a set of traditional beliefs or a traditional interpretation of "sacred history" and biblical events. "Rather it is the event itself that again and again gives rise to religious meaning, and only out of that meaning, apprehended in our own history and the history of past generations that we have made present to ourselves, do religious symbols and theological interpretations arise." Such theology as event makes the staggering claim that "it is in our lives that we apprehend the divine—not through sacred times and places and rituals alone but in the everyday happening, 'the days of our years.' " This applies even to prayer, for prayer is also an event and issues into events. For Hasidim, indeed, God himself is prayer. But that is only true when true praying *happens* as a dialogical reality.

From this it follows that legend, myth, and tale are themselves closer to religious reality than creed, doctrine, and theology—*if* one understands such tales not as illustrations of preexisting abstract ideas but as the concrete preservation of the dramatic, dialogical reality of the event. The title that Buber placed above the Hasidic tale in which Rabbi Leib comes to see the Maggid of Mezritch to watch him lace and unlace his felt shoes, "Not to Say Torah but to Be Torah," is not, as it might seem, a contrast between what a person is and what a person says. Rather, it is the basic way in which we speak to one another—through what we are. The whole person, who has brought his or her inner contradictions into some meaningful personal direction, communicates

"Torah"—instruction and guidance on the way—even by his or her most casual and unintentional acts. All of a person's gestures, utterances, and actions bear the stamp of the unique person who he or she is. This person will also teach in words, but what he or she *is* is the guarantor of what he or she *says*.

In another tale, the same Rabbi Leib contrasts apparent speaking, mere words, and real speaking, with or without words: "What does it amount to—that they expound the Torah! A man should see to it that all his actions are a Torah and that he himself becomes so entirely a Torah that one can learn from his habits and his motions and his motionless clinging to God." If this is so, not only can a unique concrete event underlie a legend, myth, or tale, but the telling of a tale may itself be an event, as when the lame disciple was healed while showing how the Baal Shem danced! The Maggid of Mezritch once said to his disciples:

> I shall teach you the best way to say Torah. You must cease to be aware of yourselves. You must be nothing but an ear which hears what the universe of the word is constantly saying within you. The moment you start hearing what you yourself are saying, you must stop.[8]

PART II

A Hasidic "Way of Life"

3

"Why Were You Not Zusya?"

Hasidism has spoken most strongly to me through *Tales of the Hasidim*—the "legendary anecdotes" that bear true witness in stammering tongue to the life of the Hasidim as Martin Buber has presented it to us. If I am asked about the uniqueness of Hasidic mysticism, I do not give a definition: I tell a tale. I can best witness, I believe, to the way in which Hasidism speaks to my condition and to the condition of my contemporaries through the tales themselves. One can find motifs in Hasidism which add up to a teaching—a way of man, a way of life. But these motifs are very closely interrelated, and they are not so much parts of a system as they are wisdom.

Hasidism emphasizes the uniqueness of each person without stressing self-realization. "When I get to heaven," said Rabbi Zusya, "they will not ask me: 'Why were you not Moses?' but 'Why were you not Zusya?' " We are called to become what we in our created uniqueness can become—not just to fulfill our social duty or realize our talent or potentialities, but to become the unique person we are called to be. This is not an already existing uniqueness that we can fulfill through "self-expression" or "self-realization." We have to realize our uniqueness in response to the world. A part of this response, for Zusya, was the fact that Moses was there for him—not as a model to imitate but as an image of the human that arose in dialogue, a "touchstone of reality" that entered into his own becoming.

"Why did you not become what only you could become?" does not mean, "Why were you not *different* from others," but "Why did you not fulfill the creative task you have become aware of as yours alone?"

> Rabbi Pinhas said: "When a man embarks on something great, in the spirit of truth, he need not be afraid that another may imitate him. But if he does not do it in the spirit of truth, but plans to do it in a way no one could imitate, then he drags the great down to the lowest level—and everyone can do the same."[1]

There is a great tendency in our culture to exalt the different and to confuse the different with the unique. The "different" is merely a term of comparison. The unique is something valued in and for itself. This is very important; for the search for originality, which is so strong in our day, usually takes the form of a different twist or a new wrinkle. What we ought to be concerned about is our faithful response. If we respond really faithfully, this will bring out our own uniqueness.

This also means, of course, that I must stand my ground and witness for that unique creation which I am. When the servant forgot to give Mendel a spoon, Rabbi Elimelech said: "Look, Mendel, you must learn to ask for a spoon and if need be, for a plate too!" This is related to the contending with God which is essential to biblical faith. "Every man should have two pockets to use as the occasion demands," said Rabbi Bunam, "in one of which are the words, 'For my sake the world was created,' and in the other the words, 'I am earth and ashes.' " This balance—neither affirming yourself absolutely nor denying yourself absolutely but recognizing that you are given a created ground on which to stand and from which to move to meet the world—is the true humility of Hasidism. "If God so desires, let him take our life," said the Rabbi of Ger, "but he must leave us that with which we love him—he must leave us our heart." Usually it is not God who takes away our heart but we ourselves—by living in such a way that there are no free moments in which our heart might open itself to the address of the world and respond. "A human being who has not a single hour for his own every day," said Rabbi Moshe Leib, "is no human being." This is for me the most painful of all the Hasidic sayings; for I encounter it again and again as a judgment on my way of life and on that of most of my contemporaries! The fact that we ourselves have chosen our form of slavery does not make it any less slavery.

To realize one's uniqueness rules out every form of imitation, even of Abraham, Isaac, and Jacob. "Each one of us in his own way shall devise something new in the light of the teachings and of service," said the Maggid (preacher) of Zlotchov, "and do what has not yet been done." When a son who inherited his father's congregation was reproached by his disciples with conducting himself differently from his father, he retorted: "I do just as my father did. He did not imitate and I do not imitate." The relationship between person and person was central to Hasidism, but only in spontaneous address and response and not in that invidious comparison and contrast that leads us to call one person "superior" to another. When someone praised one person to Rabbi Mendel of Kotzk at the expense of another, Rabbi Mendel said: "If I am I because I am I, and you are you because you are you, than I am I and you are you. But if I am I because you are you, and you are you because I am I, then I am not I, and you are not you." When Rabbi Abraham was asked why people feel so crowded despite the fact that the sages say that everything, man included, has his place, he replied: "Because each wants to occupy the place of the other."

Uniqueness does not preclude dialogue. On the contrary, it is precisely through each standing his or her own ground and yet moving to meet the other that genuine dialogue from ground to ground takes place. For a person for whom there is not dialogue, even the ground of life itself crumbles away. After the death of Rabbi Moshe of Kobryn, a friend said: "If there had been someone to whom he could have talked, he would still be alive."

When asked for one general way to the service of God, the Seer of Lublin replied:

It is impossible to tell men what way they should take. For one way to serve God is through learning, another through prayer, another through fasting, and still another through eating. Everyone should carefully observe what way his heart draws him to, and then choose this way with all his strength.[2]

Hasidism is like Hinduism in not having any one way that man should walk. But the way for the Hasid is not a matter of his caste duty, or even his dharma or karma, but of his personal uniqueness, his "I" in the deepest sense of that term. To speak of the heart drawing us does not mean the facile impulse of the moment. Our "I" is not our image of ourselves but the deepest stirring within ourselves. That stirring, in its response, becomes our *way*.

Knowledge has to do with the general. Truth has to do with the unique. The unique does not mean the different, but the particular, that which is related to for itself and as of value in itself. We will recall how the Baal Shem spoke to a group of people, and afterwards each person asserted that he had spoken to him alone, until all fell silent. The Baal Shem did not seek the least common denominator or generalities that might easily be taken in by the crowd. Rather, he spoke with such directness and concreteness that what he said addressed *each* of his hearers as the unique person he was. Rabbi Pinhas stressed that there is no person who is not incessantly being taught by his soul. "If this is so," asked one of his disciples, "why don't people obey their souls?" "The soul teaches incessantly," Rabbi Pinhas explained, "but it never repeats." The reason why the soul never repeats is that it does not teach in generalities but always only the message and demand of the unique situation in which the person finds himself.

There is, as we have seen, no *general* way to the service of God. When a woman came to Israel of Kosnitz to ask his help in bearing a son, he told her the story of a woman who had gone to the Baal Shem with a similar request. Asked what she was willing to do about it, the woman fetched her most precious possession, a fine cape. Finding the Baal Shem gone, she walked 60 versts from town to town to catch up with him and give it to him, and then the whole way back. "A year later, I was born," said Rabbi Israel. "I too will bring you a good cape of mine so that I may get a son," the woman who had come to see him cried. "That won't work," the maggid replied. "You heard the story. My mother had no story to go by."[3] The point here is not mystery or secrecy but uniqueness. The second woman wants to take the unique response of the first and turn it into a general method that can be abstracted from the situation and objectified, an *omnicompetent technique* to be applied to all situations.

Levi Yitzhak of Berditchev was once visited by an "enlightened" man who was used to looking up rabbis to debate with them and refute their old-fashioned proofs for the truth of their faith. At first Levi Yitzhak took no notice of his visitor, and then he gave him a brief glance and said, "But perhaps it is true after all!" The learned man's knees shook, for he found the zaddik terrible to behold and his simple words terrible to hear. "My son, the great Torah scholars with whom you debated wasted their words on you," Levi Yitzhak said to the man.

> When you left them you only laughed at what they had said.
> They could not set God and his kingdom on the table before you,
> and I cannot do this either. But, my son, only think! Perhaps it is
> true. Perhaps it is true after all!" The enlightened man made the
> utmost effort to reply, but the terrible "perhaps" beat on his ears
> again and again and broke down his resistance.[4]

The Enlightenment's touchstone of reality was the universal, the general, and that is how most people still regard truth today. Arguments and proofs have to do only with the general. They cannot give us the reality of a single particular. They cannot disclose the unique. The "perhaps" of Levi Yitzhak broke down the defenses of the learned man because it cut through the general possibility to the realm of the particular fact, the unique reality. Here Hasidism is very much like Zen Buddhism.

4

Serving God with the "Evil" Urge

Only if we carefully listen to what way our heart draws us, can we discover our unique way and follow it with all our strength. Yet often we are cut off from the awareness of our own deepest self and do not hear the call of the heart. That is why the "evil" urge is so important to Hasidism.

In the Book of Genesis this word for "urge" appears as "imaginings." The Lord gives as his reason for destroying the world by flood, "For the imaginings of man's heart are evil from his youth onward." Yet after the Flood, this same reason is given for never again destroying the world by flood. For these same "imaginings," although evil from youth on, *can* be directed to God. Similarly, the Talmud says man must love God with *both* urges, the good and the "evil." Without the evil urge, no man could have a business or raise a family. That means the "evil" urge is not evil in itself. It is evil only when it is not given direction. It is evil only when it is not given the personal meaning of our unique response to the situation. It is needed for our service. The person who succeeds in being "good" by repressing the "evil" urge is not serving God with all his or her heart, soul, and might. The "evil" urge is the passion, the power which is given us to serve

God. We cannot extirpate it or do away with it. When it seems to make us fail, it does so because we have tried to impose upon ourselves and our environment what we are determined to be.

The "evil" urge is that something more in us that taps us on the shoulder and recalls us to ourselves. Often we have so lost touch with ourselves that we do not know which way our heart draws us. It is then that precisely the "evil" urge which seems to wish to lead us astray comes to our rescue. By its very tempting of us, it tells us that we have left ourselves out of our own projects, that our deepest passion has not been given direction, that our decisions have not been made with our whole being.

"He who still harbors an evil urge is at great advantage," said one Hasidic rabbi, "for he can serve God with it. He can gather all his passion and warmth and pour them into the service of God. . . . What counts is to restrain the blaze in the hour of desire and let it flow into the hours of prayer and service." This does not mean the repression of desire, but giving it meaningful direction.

The "evil" urge was thus potentially good to the Hasidim; yet they had no illusions about its being an easy matter to give the "evil" urge direction. The Maggid of Mezritch was recognized as the successor to the Baal Shem because he answered the question of how man can break pride by saying that no one can break it: "We must struggle with it all the days of our life." Similarly, the Rabbi of Rishyn said to a young man who wanted help in breaking his evil impulse: "You will break your back and your hip, yet you will not break an impulse. But if you pray and learn and work in all seriousness, the evil in your impulses will vanish of itself." Sometimes the result is more of a draw, as when Rabbi Moshe of Kobryn compared the service of God to walking over a freshly plowed field in which furrows alternate with ridges: "Now you go up, now you go down, now the Evil Urge gets a hold on you, now you get a hold on him. Just you see to it that it is you who deal the last blow!"

You cannot get a hold on the evil urge through self-mortification, however. The Maggid of Koznitz said to a man who wore nothing but a sack and fasted from one Sabbath to the next, "The Evil Urge is tricking you into that sack. He who pretends to fast . . . but secretly eats a little something every day, is spiritually better off than you, for he is only deceiving others, while you are deceiving yourself."

When another Hasid, known for the harsh penances he imposed on himself, came to visit the Maggid of Zlotchov, the latter said to him: "Yudel, you are wearing a hair shirt against your flesh. If you were not given to sudden anger, you would not need it, and since you are given to sudden anger, it will not help you."

Worse and more harmful than the sin a man plunges into when he gives way to the evil urge is the despondency which overtakes him by way of his sinning. Once he sees himself as a sinner, then the evil urge really has him in its power. Instead of sinning and then saying, "But I won't sin again," like the cheerful sinner of whom the Seer of Lublin was so fond, he gives way to the image of himself as a sinner and loses what resources he might have had to direct the evil urge in the service of God.

The power of the evil urge is the power of desire—desire for something that turns out to be nothing. The Evil Urge goes around the world with his fist closed, and everyone thinks that in that fist is just what he wants most in the world and follows after it. But the Evil Urge opens his fist, and it is empty. Once some disciples of Rabbi Pinhas ceased talking in embarrassment when he entered the House of Study. When he asked them what they were talking about, they said: "Rabbi, we were saying how afraid we are that the Evil Urge will pursue us." "Don't worry," he replied. "You have not gotten high enough for it to pursue you. For the time being, you are still pursuing it." This is how it is with most of us. Like the man who complained to the Seer of Lublin that he was disturbed by "alien thoughts," our search for every variety of excitement, titillation, ego aggrandizement, or pleasure are just "our own usual thoughts." We are running after the "Evil Urge," rather than it after us.

Passion means that one does not suppress one's humanity before bringing oneself into relation with others but, on the contrary, directs one's "evil" urge into that relationship in such a way that, without losing its force, it ceases to be evil. It is in this sense that Hasidism represents a sanctification of the profane in which every natural urge is waiting to be hallowed and the profane itself just a name for what has not yet become open to the holy.

This concrete and realistic approach to the "evil urge" is

vividly illustrated by a story of the Baal Shem's called "The Limits of Advice." When the disciples of the Baal Shem asked him how to know whether a celebrated scholar whom they proposed to visit was a true zaddik, he answered:

> Ask him to advise you what to do to keep unholy thoughts from disturbing you in your prayers and studies. If he gives you advice, then you will know that he belongs to those who are of no account. For this is the service of men in the world to the very hour of their death; to struggle time after time with the extraneous, and time after time to uplift and fit it into the nature of the Divine Name.[1]

So often the religious is conceived of as putting aside the extraneous and the profane and turning to the holy and the pure. But here the extraneous is precisely that which has something to ask of us. Once a group of Hasidim started to pray in one place and then went to another, at which the first place cried out: "What is wrong with me that you went to another place? And if I am evil, is it not up to you to redeem me?"

Jesus offered his disciples a counsel of perfection—"But I say unto you that he who looks at a woman to lust after her in his heart has already committed adultery." Paul, in contrast, saw not only temptation but sin as inevitable—"Of myself (in my flesh) I can do no good thing." "The evil that I would not do I do." In between the teaching that man can overcome temptation altogether and become "pure in heart" and that which sees man as naturally sinful is the teaching, already present in the Bible and the Talmud, but given strongest emphasis and exemplification in Hasidism, that the daily renewal of creation also means the daily renewal of temptation and with it the strength and the grace to direct that temptation into the service of God through an essential and meaningful relation with the world.

If the Hasidic hallowing of the everyday is of importance in contrast with Christianity, it is of still greater importance in contrast with gnosticism. Common to the ancient Christian and non-Christian Gnostics and to the more recent gnostical movements in Judaism associated with the pseudo-messiahs Sabbatai Zvi and Jacob Frank, is substituting for the task of hallowing an as yet unhallowed creation, the doctrine that within the community of the "elect" everything is already holy.

While antinomian gnosticism rejects creation in general as radically evil and incapable of being hallowed, it holds that its members, particularly the so-called perfect or elect, are so holy that not only are they allowed to sin, but positively should do so, in order to raise sin itself to holiness. Revolting against the distinction between good and evil, the radical Sabbatians and the Frankists, two pseudo-messianic Jewish movements of the seventeenth and eighteenth centuries, believed that they could redeem evil by performing it as if it were not evil, that is, by preserving an inner intention of purity in contrast to the deed. This illusion, divested of the weird and exotic costume of the Sabbatian and Frankist orgies, has a decidedly modern ring.

> Instead of making reality the starting point of life, reality that is full of cruel contradictions but just thereby calling forth true greatness, namely the quiet work of overcoming the contradictions, one surrenders to illusion, intoxicates oneself in it, subjugates life to it. In the same measure in which one does this, the core of his existence becomes burning and unfruitful at once, he becomes at once completely agitated and crippled in his motive power.[2]

This demonic "lust for overrunning reality" is not simply a product of unbelief but a crisis within people's souls, a crisis of temptation, freedom, and dishonesty in which "the realms are overturned, everything encroaches on everything else, and possibility is more powerful than reality." The fascination with the demonic in modern literature, the tendency of many to turn psychoanalysis or "psychodrama" into a cult of self-realization, the illusory belief that personal fulfillment can come through "release" of one's deep inward energies, and the more specific forms of modern gnosticism, such as the analytic psychology of Carl Jung, which on occasion advocates taking part in evil as the road to the integration of the self—all these show the peculiarly modern relevance of this "crisis of temptation and dishonesty." "Behind the demonic mask one imagines that the countenance of divine freedom is to be discovered; one does not let oneself be deluded by the temptations, but one also does not drive them out."[3]

Hasidism offers a teaching that rejects both the radical separation of good and evil and the confusion of the two. But this teaching can only become ours if it is lifted out of the realm of spiritual inspiration, and realized concretely in our interhuman relationships.

Although Hasidism stands squarely on the doctrines of both the *Zohar* and the Lurianic kabbalah, it shapes their attitudes toward bodily life into a pervasive, practical teaching of the sanctifying of the profane and, for the branch of Hasidism that stayed close to the Baal Shem Tov, the "hallowing of the everyday." This teaching of hallowing the everyday has been given concentrated expression by Martin Buber in his little classic *The Way of Man According to the Teachings of Hasidism:*

> By no means . . . can it be our true task, in the world into which we have been set, to turn away from the things and beings that we meet on our way and that attract our hearts; our task is precisely to get in touch, by hallowing our relationship with them, with what manifests itself in them as beauty, pleasure, enjoyment. Hasidism teaches that rejoicing in the world, if we hallow it with our whole being, leads to rejoicing in God . . . Any natural act, if hallowed, leads to God, and nature needs man for what no angel can perform on it, namely, its hallowing.[4]

We human beings have been placed in the world that we may raise the dust to the spirit. Our task, as long as we live, is to "struggle with the extraneous and uplift and fit it into the divine Name." All sacraments have at their core a natural activity taken from the natural course of life that is consecrated in them. But the heart of the sacrament is equally that it does not level the event down to a symbolic gesture or mystically exalt it to "an exuberantly heartfelt point," but that it "includes an elementary, life-claiming and life-determining experience of the *other,* the otherness, as of something coming to meet one and acting toward one." Therefore, it is not merely "celebrated" or "experienced." It seizes and claims the human being in the core of his wholeness and needs nothing less than his wholeness in order to endure it. This otherness with which one comes into contact is a material or corporeal one; for "there is no rung of human life on which we cannot find the holiness of God everywhere and at all times."[5]

All of the characteristic attitudes of Hasidism toward bodily life can be understood in terms of this teaching: the relation of body and soul, learning from the actions and gestures of the zaddik, shaping matter and refining flesh, connecting earth and heaven, and the Hasidic attitudes toward asceticism, eating, and sex. The true Hasid "makes his body the throne of the life-soul and the life-soul the throne of the heart and the heart the throne of the spirit and the spirit the throne of the light of the indwelling glory." "If a man of Israel has himself firmly in hand, and stands solidly on the earth, then his head reaches up to heaven." Schneur Zalman of Ladi answered his son's question as to what he prayed with by saying, "With the floor and the bench."[6] Commenting on this, Buber writes:

> Everything wants to be hallowed, to be brought into the holy, everything worldly in its worldliness: it does not want to be stripped of its worldliness, it wants to be brought in its worldliness into the *kavana* [intention] of the redemption—everything wants to become sacrament. The creature, the things seek us out on our paths; what comes to meet us on our way needs us for its way. "With the floor and the bench" shall one pray; they want to come to us, everything wants to come to us, everything wants to come to God through us. What concern of ours, if they exist, are the upper worlds! Our concern is "in this lower world, the world of corporeality, to let the hidden life of God shine forth."[7]

The service that the human being must perform each day anew is to shape matter into form, refine the flesh, and let the light penetrate the darkness, *until the darkness itself shines,* and there is no longer any division between the two. Here is a dialectical rather than a dualistic attitude toward the interrelation of body and soul, body and spirit. As one Hasidic master put it:

> Everyone should have pity upon his body and allow it to share in all that illumines the soul. We must purify the body very greatly so that it may share in everything the soul receives, so that there may be a change in the present state where the soul attains to lofty matters and the body knows nothing about them. But if the body is given a share, it can also be of use to the soul. For, at times, the soul falls from its rung, and then the purified body can help it up again through the power of the light it has absorbed. That is why Job says: "From out of my flesh shall I see God."[8]

The Hasidic teaching of the ultimate unity of body and soul also determines its attitude toward asceticism. In contrast to other religions, and even to many Kabbalists, for whom asceticism is considered a goal in itself, for Hasidism it is never more than a means whereby some persons achieve liberation from their enslavement to the world, deepest heart-searching, and ultimate communion with the Absolute. "Never should asceticism gain mastery over a man's life. A man may only detach himself from nature in order to revert to it again and, in hallowed contact with it, find his way back to God."

The Baal Shem took six loaves and a pitcher of water with him when he went into seclusion for a week. When he was ready to go home at the end of the week, he lifted his sack, felt how heavy it was, and, opening it, found to his great surprise that all the loaves were still in it. "Fasting such as this, is allowed!" The Baal Shem taught that whoever mortifies his flesh will have to render account as a sinner, because he has tormented his soul. Similarly, the Baal Shem's great disciple, the Maggid of Mezritch, taught that the soul can endure the body and need not separate from it. One ought not to mortify the body; for the soul shall not abhor the body. One of the later zaddikim saw self-mortification as worse than the hypocrisy of him who pretends to fast from Sabbath to Sabbath but secretly eats a little something every day; the latter is only deceiving others while the former is deceiving himself.

One young man who fasted from Sabbath to Sabbath and only with repeated difficulty overcame the temptation to take a drink of water was greeted by his master with the word "patchwork!" This was not because his master was partial to asceticism but because he understood that one can only do some unusual work with a united soul. *The soul here means the whole person,* body and spirit together; for only a person, no part of whose physical being remains outside of his action, can perform *work that is all of a piece.* "The soul is not really united, unless all bodily energies, all the limbs of the body, are united."

The finest manifestation of this unity of body and soul is the Hasidic teaching that one should learn from every limb of the zaddik. The Great Maggid was depicted by Hasidic legend as a person who had purified and unified his body and spirit so utterly that his body was as his spirit and his spirit was as his body. One Hasid who was lame, as we have seen, related how the holy Baal

Shem used to hop and dance while he prayed and was so swept away by his own story that he himself began to hop and dance and from that hour was cured of his lameness. One zaddik declared that he did not want the rungs of the spirit without the garment of the flesh, i.e., the guidance of his teacher after he was dead; for that is the mystery of the Divine Presence in exile. Another told of how, when he visited a fellow zaddik, the holy old man examined him limb by limb, from head to toe, the way a cooper examines a cask.

The Hasidic enthusiasm for being all of a piece extended beyond our ordinary conceptions. Rabbi Shlomo of Karlin always held a piece of sugar in his hand when he drank tea or coffee. When his son asked him about it, he handed the piece of sugar to his son who tasted it and discovered, with astonishment, that there was no sweetness left in it at all. "A man in whom everything is unified can taste with his hand as if with his tongue," the son later explained.

We have noted how Rabbi Hayyim of Krosno became absorbed in the spectacle of a rope dancer. To walk the rope, the man had to be all of a piece, and that is what the zaddikim desired for their disciples as well as themselves. Rabbi Mendel of Kotzk saw to it that his Hasidim wore nothing around the neck while praying. "For," he said, "there must be no break between the heart and the brain."

This wholeness of body and soul in the unified person is attained by the zaddik and the Hasidim not through aiming at the self or at the realization of their potentialities, but through becoming whole in dialogue with others and with God.

Rabbi Israel of Kosnitz was in poor health from childhood on, so much so that the doctors were surprised that he stayed alive. But when he came into prayer, he was transformed and walked with light and quick step, and when he went to a circumcision, he sprang into the carriage, exchanging his strength for God's, who "has strength to spare!"

Every week on the day before the Sabbath, around the hour of noon, the Baal Shem's heart began to beat so loudly that everyone with him could hear it. Once the Baal Shem said to his body: "I am surprised, body, that you have not crumbled to bits for fear of your Maker!"

When Rabbi Elimelekh of Lishensk was sunk in the contemplation of the awfulness of God, his arteries grew as stiff as hard ropes, and the artery behind the ear, "which stirs at nothing in the world, and does not tremble until the hour of death," day after day throbbed with a strong pulse.

Becoming whole means to give direction to one's passions, and giving direction to one's passions means to serve God with the "evil" urge. The "evil" urge is the passion or desire which, if left undirected, *becomes* evil, but which, if brought into the dialogue with God, is an essential ingredient of human wholeness.

Hallowing, for the Baal Shem, did not just mean that in the performance of natural acts one concentrated on special mystical meditations, as it did for so many of the Lurian Kabbalists and of the Hasidic masters who followed them. It meant that the action was in itself meaningful and, when performed with the whole being, was itself hallowed:

> Take care that all that you do for God's sake be itself service of God. Thus eating: do not say that the intention of eating shall be that you gain strength for the service of God. This is also a good intention, of course; but the true perfection only exists where the deed itself happens to heaven, that is where the holy sparks are raised.[9]

Those who are familiar with contemporary Hasidic men, who shun most contact with women for fear of succumbing to the "evil" urge, will be surprised to learn how different was the classical Hasidic attitude toward sex. Instead of being an evil to be feared, it was seen as one of the chief ways by which human beings can serve God and hallow the everyday. The Hasidim not only continued the Kabbalistic use of sexual imagery to portray the relation of the procreative and the receptive elements of God and creation. They also saw sex as a metaphor of man's intercourse with God. In his "Instructions in Intercourse with God" the Baal Shem used human sexual intercourse in its most explicit form as the parable for praying:

> Prayer is a coupling with the Glory of God. Therefore man should move himself up and down at the beginning of prayer, but then he can stand unmoved and cleave to God in a great cleaving. And

because he moves, he can attain to a great awakening so that he must reflect: Why do I move up and down? Certainly, because the Glory of God stands over against me. And over this he enters into a great rapture.

This metaphor is extended into the connection between sexual intercourse and conception.

"In my flesh," says Job, "I shall see God."
As in bodily coupling, only he can beget who uses a living limb with longing and joy, so in the spiritual coupling, that is, with the speaker of the teaching and of the prayer, it is he who performs them with living limb in joy and bliss who begets.

The Baal Shem also compares prayer to the wedding and the lovemaking that follows. At the wedding the bride is clothed in all kinds of garments, "but when the nuptials themselves are to take place, the garments are taken from her in order that the bodies can come close to each other." Prayer, similarly, is "the bride who at first is adorned with many garments, but then, when her friend embraces her, all clothing is taken from her." In another extended conceit the Baal Shem expands on the belief that if the power of procreation first stirs in the woman, a male child is born. From this he suggests that the beginning in the dialogue with God is up to us. "If the movement first awakens from below, then the divine quality of mercy prevails," the masculine being, in Hebrew, as opposed to other languages, the symbol of mercy.[10]

To Hasidism, as to the Lurian kabbalah, the coupling of man and wife is itself a sacral act, one of the chief ways by which the human being hallows existence. Thus Buber expounds:

Even when it is only two human beings who consecrate themselves to each other sacramentally in marriage, in brotherhood—that other covenant, the covenant between the Absolute and the concrete, is secretly consummated; for the consecration does not come from the power of the human partners, but from the eternal wings that overshadow both. Everything unconditional into which men enter with each other receives its strength from the presence of the unconditional.[11]

To the Baal Shem, the sacrament of marriage was so totally a body-soul reality that after his wife died, he said: "I thought that a storm would sweep me up to Heaven like Elijah. But now that I am only half a body, this is no longer possible."[12]

Since Hasidic hallowing included the whole of corporeal life, sleep too was seen as a service to God. Because he did not want to interrupt his studies for too long, Rabbi Shmelke always slept sitting up, with his head resting on his arm and in his fingers a lit candle which roused him when the flame touched his hand.

> When Rabbi Elimelekh visited him and recognized the power of the holiness which was still locked within him, he prepared a couch for him and with great difficulty persuaded him to lie down for a little while. Then he closed and shuttered the windows. Rabbi Shmelke slept until broad daylight . . . [and] he was filled with a hitherto unknown sunny clearness.

When he prayed before the congregation, they were entranced and uplifted by the manifest power of his holiness:

> When he recited the verses about the Red Sea, they gathered up the hems of their kaftans for fear the waves towering to the left and right might wet them with salty foam. Later Shmelke said to Elimelekh: "Not until this day did I know that one can also serve God with sleep."

Rabbi Elimelekh was also the master of the Seer of Lublin whose disciple in turn was the "Holy Yehudi." When asked what he had learned from the Seer, the Yehudi replied: "When I get into bed, I fall asleep on the instant." Rabbi Menahem Mendel of Vorki declared that he was more pleased by the "honest sleep" of the people who were sleeping on the floor of the House of Study than with the noise of those who were studying at the tables.[13]

The Hasidic concern for the bodily life was also, of course, a concern for right movement, for rhythm, for tempo. Once Levi Yitzhak of Berditchev met a man hurrying along the street, looking neither to the left nor to the right. When he asked the man why he was rushing so, the man replied: "I am after my livelihood."

> "And how do you know," continued the rabbi, "that your livelihood is running on before you, so that you have to rush after it?

Perhaps it is behind you, and all you need do to encounter it is to stand still—but you are running away from it!"[14]

The Baal Shem combined into a single flame the fire of corporeal passion and the light of spiritual holiness. After the death of the Baal Shem, his son saw him in the shape of a fiery mountain, which burst into countless sparks. When his son asked the Baal Shem why he appeared in a shape such as this, the Baal Shem replied: "In this shape I served God."

Rabbi Yehiel Mikhal of Zlotchov interpreted the biblical injunction to "Be fruitful and multiply" as meaning that we must be *more* than the animals—by walking upright, clinging to God, and consecrating our cohabitation to him. God forgave David after he sinned with Bathsheba, said Rabbi Shalom Shakhna of Probishtch, because he returned to God and said his psalm with the same passion with which he had gone to Bathsheba. The service that we must perform all of our days, said Rabbi Israel of Rizhyn, is "to shape matter into form, to refine the flesh, and to let the light penetrate the darkness until the darkness itself shines and there is no longer any division between the two." Rabbi Bunam once discovered that a young man whom he was looking after had slipped away from him and gone into a brothel. Entering the brothel, Bunam asked the girl at the piano to sing her best selection, and thus drew the youth out of the room he had retired into. In the next days Rabbi Bunam recited psalms with such great force that he "extricated the youth completely from the power of materiality," and brought him to the point of perfect turning. "That time in the brothel," Bunam told his friends years later, "I learned that the Divine Presence can descend anywhere."[15]

In extension of the Hasidic teaching of the hallowing of the everyday, Buber once commented that the profane is just that which has not yet been sanctified. There is nothing which is inherently profane, nothing so extraneous that it cannot be brought into our dialogue with God. There are no words or actions in themselves which are useless, said Rabbi Pinhas of Koretz, but one can make them useless by saying or doing them uselessly. "All joys hail from paradise," said Rabbi Pinhas, "and jests too, provided they are uttered in true joy." Even the Evil Urge wants to become good by driving the human being to overcome it, and to make it good. What it is actually saying to the person it is trying to seduce, said Rabbi Mikhal of Zlotchov, is: "Let us leave this disgraceful state and take service with the Creator, so that I too may go and mount with you rung by rung, although I seem to oppose, to disturb, and hinder you."[16]

For this reason the zaddikim saw value in what the ordinary "religious" person shuns as the secular or profane world. When a Hasid complained to Rabbi Zev Wolf of Zbarazh that some persons were turning night into day playing cards, Rabbi Wolf pointed out that by learning to stay awake and persist in their card playing, they were learning how to serve God. "All they need do is turn to God—and what excellent servants they will make for him then!" Rabbi Levi Yitzhak of Berditchev grabbed the coat of a great sinner and said, "Sir, I envy you. When you turn to God you will shine with great splendor."[17]

The Seer of Lublin conversed at length with a great sinner whenever the man wanted to because, as he explained to his disciples, he loved gaiety and hated dejection: "Others repent the moment they have sinned, are sorry for a moment, and then return to their folly. But he knows no regrets and no doldrums, and lives in his happiness as in a tower. And it is the radiance of his happiness that overwhelms my heart." Rabbi Israel of Rizhyn distinguished between those zaddikim who studied and prayed all day and held themselves far from lowly concerns in order to attain holiness, and those whose concerns are not themselves but all lowly things, because they want to deliver the holy sparks in all things back to God.[18]

From all this it follows that the zaddikim urged their Hasidim not to dwell on sin. Asked why we recite our sins in alphabetical order on the Day of Atonement, Rabbi Yitzhak of Vorki replied that that is the only way we know when to stop beating our breasts. "For there is no end to sin, and no end to the awareness of sin, but there *is* an end to the alphabet."[19] What Rabbi Yitzhak of Vorki said tersely, Rabbi Yitzhak Meir of Ger said at length in *A Sermon:*

> He who has done ill and talks about it and thinks about it all the time does not cast the base thing he did out of his thoughts, and whatever one thinks, therein one is; one's soul is wholly and utterly in what one thinks, and so such a man dwells in baseness. He will

certainly not be able to turn, for his spirit will grow coarse and his heart stubborn, and in addition to this he may be overcome by gloom. What would you? Rake the muck this way, rake the muck that way—it will always be muck. Have I sinned, or have I not sinned—what does Heaven get out of it? In the time I am brooding over it, I could be stringing pearls for the delight of Heaven. That is why it is written: "Depart from evil and do good"—turn wholly away from evil, do not dwell upon it, and do good. You have done wrong? Then counteract it by doing right.[20]

Not only sin, evil, and the extraneous can be sanctified, but also the neutral, the banal, the seemingly indifferent, the everyday. Once, on a journey, the Baal Shem heard of a hose maker who went daily to the House of Prayer, even if a minyan, a quorum of 10 worshipers, was not present. The Baal Shem asked that the man be brought to him and, when the latter obliged, out of respect for the Baal Shem, questioned him about his work. Before he went to pray, he confided, he made hose and, while he made them, recited the psalms which he knew by heart. After the hose maker had left, the Baal Shem said to his disciples, "Today you have seen the cornerstone which will uphold the Temple until the Messiah comes."[21]

The Baal Shem's grandson, Rabbi Barukh of Mezbizh, stressed that right service means that no matter what fires of ecstasy a person feels within him, he should not allow the flame to burst from the vessel, but perform every tangible action in the manner proper to it. To a Hasid who asked God for his livelihood so he might better serve God, Rabbi Shlomo of Karlin said, "What God really wants of you is not study or prayer, but the sighs of your heart, which is breaking because the travail of gaining a livelihood hinders you in the service of God."

5

Kavana
Bringing Oneself as an Offering

*H*ow does man serve God with the "evil" urge? Not through turning away from everyday life in the world, but through bringing right dedication—*kavana*—to everything one does, through responding with one's whole being to the unique claim of unique situations. This means bringing all of one's passion into meaningful relationship with the people one meets and the situations one encounters. Even the right mood is of no avail if the motivation is wrong: The person who prays in sorrow because of the bleakness which burdens his spirit does not know the real fear of God, and the person who prays in joy because of the radiance of his spirit does not know the love of God. His "fear is the burden of sadness, and his love is nothing but empty joy." Honest grief, in contrast, is that of a person who knows what he lacks, while the truly joyful person, as we have seen, is like someone whose house has burned down and who begins to build anew out of the deep need of his soul: "Over every stone that is laid, his heart rejoices."

Once the Maggid of Mezritch let a sigh escape when, as a young man, he was poor and his baby was too weak even to cry. Instantly a voice said, "You have lost your share in the world to come." "Good," exclaimed the Maggid. "Now I can begin to serve in good earnest!'' *Kavana* does not mean that what is important is "purity of heart," but that one must bring oneself with all one's possibility of response into every action. This is the Hasidic image of the human: "Only he who brings himself to the Lord as an offering may be called man." This bringing oneself is no once-for-all commitment, but an ever-renewed finding of direction, a responding to the call in each new hour.

The Lurian kabbalah taught that originally there were vessels so full of grace that they burst and sparks of light descended into the darkness and were covered with shells. We can help restore these sparks to their divine source and thus take part in the Messianic restoration of the exiled Shekinah to God. To the Lurian Kabbalist, and to many of the zaddikim who came after the Baal Shem, this act of *tikkun,* or restoration, was made possible through special magical and mystical intentions *(kavanot).* To the Baal Shem and those zaddikim who remained faithful to his tradition, the *kavanot* were less important than *kavana,* the consecration and dedication of the whole being that comes in the turning to God *(teshuvah):*

> In all that is in the world dwell holy sparks, no thing is empty of them. In the actions of men also, indeed even in the sins that a man does, dwell holy sparks of the glory of God. And what is it that the sparks await that dwell in the sins? It is the turning. In the hour where you turn on account of sin, you raise to the higher world the sparks that were in it.[1]

We would not today use a mythical image such as that of the sparks, but we try to convey the same thing by our modern myths, such as process, flowing, energy, development, evolution. The Hasidim did not see the body or the food for the body as mere substance but as divine pulsating and living energy:

> In the course of the sabbath meal Rabbi Moshe once took a piece of bread in his hand and said to his hasidim: "It is written: 'Man doth not live by bread only, but by every thing that proceedeth out of the mouth of the Lord doth man live.' The life of man is not sustained by the stuff of bread but by the sparks of divine life that are within it. He is here. All exists because of his life-giving life,

and when he withdraws from anything, it crumbles away to nothing."[2]

We eat not just for the sake of our nourishment but to liberate
the divine sparks in the food. It is not our self-realization but our
contact with all creatures and things that is the goal of human
existence. A striking example of this reversal of the ordinary per-
spective is Rabbi Barukh's teaching that medicine is not so much
there for our sake as we for its sake:

> Once Rabbi Barukh went to the city and bought medicine for
> his sick daughter. The servant set it on the windowsill of his room
> in the inn. Rabbi Barukh went up and down, looked at the little
> bottles, and said: "If it is God's will that my daughter Raizel re-
> cover, she needs no medicine. But if God made his miraculous
> power manifest to all eyes, then no one would, any longer, have
> freedom of choice: everyone would know. But God wanted men
> to have a choice, so he cloaked his doing in the courses of Nature.
> That is why he created healing herbs." Then he walked up and
> down the room again, and asked: "But why does one give poisons
> to the sick?" And answered: "The 'sparks' that fell from the pri-
> meval iniquity of the worlds into the 'shells' and penetrated the
> stuff of stones, plants, and animals—all ascend back to their source
> through the sanctification of the devout who work at them, use
> them, and consume them in holiness. But how shall those sparks
> that fell into bitter poisons and poisonous herbs, be redeemed?
> That they might not remain in exile, God appointed them for the
> sick: to each the carriers of the sparks which belongs to the root
> of his soul. Thus the sick are themselves physicians who heal the
> poisons."[3]

One thing Hasidism, Zen Buddhism, Sufi mysticism, and the
Catholic Franciscans have in common, as Martin Buber has
pointed out, is that in all of them there prevailed the hallowing
of life through devotion to the divine. In Hasidism and in Hasidism
alone, however, it is not the life of monks that is reported, but
that of spiritual leaders who are married and produce children and
who stand at the head of communities composed of families. "In
Hasidism the hallowing extends fundamentally to the natural and
social life. Here alone the whole man, as God has created him,
enters into the hallowing." In this connection Buber makes a fun-

damental distinction that his critics, such as Gershom Scholem and Rivka Schatz-Uffenheimer, have failed to make between two kinds of zaddikim, those who hold to the essentially Gnostic view that one must lift oneself out of the "corporeal" reality of human life into the "nothing" of pure spirit in order to attain contact with God, and those who believe that *devekut,* cleaving to or constant being with God, is reached through human beings dedicating to God all that is lived by them.

The first stream originated in the Maggid of Mezritch, but before that, *devekut,* as the hallowing of all life, originated with his teacher, the Baal Shem Tov. No contest between these two views took place in Hasidism, but Buber sets them in contrast, characterizing the stream of hallowing, which he elsewhere calls *devotio,* as the primal faith of Israel, and the stream of nullification as "the hypertrophy of mystical-magical doctrine." The Baal Shem included everything corporeal without exception in the sphere of what can be hallowed through *kavana,* or intention, not excluding the coupling of man and wife. "Of a 'nullification' of the concrete there is in *this* line of Hasidism—which begins with its beginning—nothing to be found." The raising of the divine "sparks" from the beings and the things is no annihilation, but rather dedication, hallowing, transformation without suspension of concreteness. When the Baal Shem says, "In the hour when on account of sin you carry out the turning, you raise the sparks that were in it into the upper world," that is no nullification, but a bridge-building.

Therefore, Buber's selection from Hasidism "necessarily directed itself to the unjustly despised 'anecdotes'—stories of lived life—and 'aphorisms'—sayings in which life documents itself." For both expressed with great pregnancy the life of the zaddikim. Some zaddikim were predominantly teachers of future zaddikim; others, like Levi Yitzhak of Berditchev, Rabbi Zusya, and Rabbi Moshe Leib of Sasov, were popular figures who helped the broad circle of followers among the Hasidim. These latter represent the simply unique in Hasidism. The relationship of the master to the disciples has also perhaps taken exemplary shape in the writings of Zen Buddhism, but that of the master to ignorant people is nowhere in the world expressed as it is here.[4]

Two of the tales themselves clearly express the contrast which

Buber makes between the *kavanot*—the special magical and mystical intentions which Hasidism inherited from the Lurian kabbalah—and *kavana*—the dedication or consecration of the whole being in all of one's actions. Once the Baal Shem asked his disciple Rabbi Wolf Kitzes to learn the *kavanot* of blowing the ram's horn, the shofar, so that, on New Year's Day, he might announce before him the order of sounds. Rabbi Wolf wrote them down on a slip of paper which he lost, due, it was said, to the work of the Baal Shem. When he tried to remember the *kavanot,* he found that he had forgotten everything and, weeping, he announced the order of sounds quite simply without referring to the *kavanot.* "There are many halls in the king's palace," the Baal Shem later said to him, "and intricate keys open the doors, but the axe is stronger than all of these, and no bolt can withstand it. What are all *kavanot* compared to one really heartfelt grief!"[5]

The other tale comes from Rabbi Moshe of Kobryn, one of the later masters. Speaking to an author who questioned him about the kabbala and the *kavanot,* Rabbi Moshe said:

> "You must keep in mind that the word Kabbalah is derived from *Kabbel:* to accept; and the word kavvanah from *Kavven:* to direct. For the ultimate significance of all the wisdom of the Kabbalah is to accept the yoke of the Kingdom of God, and the ultimate significance of all the art of the *kavanot* is to direct one's heart to God."[6]

In his Introduction to *The Early Masters,* Buber speaks of the Baal Shem as "the infinitely rare and decisive phenomenon: the union of fire and light in a human being," the "union within a person of heavenly light and earthly fire," through which the Baal Shem testified in his life to the divine unity of spirit and nature from which alone true ecstasy hails. When the Maggid of Mezritch begged Heaven to show him a man whose every limb and fiber was holy, he was shown the form of the Baal Shem Tov, which was all of fire with no shred of substance in it. "When I weld my spirit to God, I let my mouth say what it will," said the Baal Shem, "for then all my words are bound to their root in Heaven." At first the Baal Shem cleaved so wholly to God that he did not know how to talk to people. But then Ahijah the prophet taught him verses of the Psalms which enabled him to talk to people without disrupting his clinging to God.[7]

Heschel, the Apter rebbe, linked hallowing of the everyday with freedom of choice. In the days of the Temple there was the death penalty, whipping, and later Israel had penal codes; so there was no freedom. "But now everyone can sin openly and without shame, and prosper. And so whoever leads a good life today is worthy in the eyes of God, and redemption depends on him."

Rabbi Moshe of Kobryn, as we have seen, interpreted God's statement to Moses, "Put off thy shoes from thy feet" to mean that every person should put off the habitual in order to know that the place in which he is standing is holy ground, or, as Martin Buber and Franz Rosenzweig translated it, "the ground of hallowing." "For there is no rung of human life on which we cannot find the holiness of God everywhere and at all times."

"To what purpose was man created?" Mendel once asked a disciple, who replied, "So that he might perfect his soul." "No, indeed!" retorted the Kotzker. "Man was created so that he might lift up the Heavens." We might protest that the Heavens do not need lifting up, but it is precisely how we live on earth and hallow the everyday that raises them. Once the Kotzker rebbe surprised a group of learned men by asking, "Where is the dwelling of God?" "What a thing to ask!" they laughed at him. "Is not the whole world full of his glory!" But the Kotzker said, "God dwells wherever man lets him in."[8] Buber's comment on this tale at the end of his classic little work *The Way of Man According to the Teachings of the Hasidim,* is too relevant to hallowing the everyday to leave unquoted here:

> This is the ultimate purpose: to let God in. But we can let him in only where we really stand, where we live, where we live a true life. If we maintain holy intercourse with the little world entrusted to us, if we help the holy spiritual substance to accomplish itself in that section of Creation in which we are living, then we are establishing, in this our place, a dwelling for the Divine Presence.[9]

"The hallowing of the world will be this letting-in," Buber comments in *Hasidism and Modern Man,* and supplements it by an unfolding of another teaching of the Kotzker, one which we have already seen, namely that the biblical injunction "Ye shall be holy men unto me" really means: "Ye shall be holy unto me, but as men, ye shall be humanly holy unto me":

> If man can become "humanly holy," i.e., become holy as man, and, indeed, as it is written, "to Me," i.e., in the face of God, then he, the individual man, can also—in the measure of his personal ability and in the manner of his personal possibility—become one in the sight of God. Man cannot approach the divine by reaching beyond the human; he can approach Him through becoming human. To become human is what he, this individual man, has been created for. This, so it seems to me, is the eternal core of Hasidic life and of Hasidic teaching.[10]

To hallow the everyday means then to make oneself holy. Rabbi Barukh rephrased the words of the psalm, "I will not give sleep to mine eyes, nor slumber to mine eyelids until I find out a place for the Lord," to read, "Until I find myself and make myself a place to be ready for the descending of the Divine Presence." Rabbi Pinhas said that God is called *makom*, or place, because "Man should go into God, so that God may surround him and become his place." "If a man of Israel has himself firmly in hand, and stands solidly on the earth," said Rabbi Aaron of Karlin, "then his head reaches up to Heaven." Asked what he had learned from his teacher, the Great Maggid, Rabbi Aaron replied that he had learned nothing at all, i.e., the meaning of nothingness: "I learned that I am nothing at all, and that I AM, notwithstanding." "The worst thing the Evil Urge can achieve," said Rabbi Shlomo of Karlin, is "to make man forget that he is the son of a king."[11]

Early Christianity regarded the world as a place of sin and temptation and called the Devil the Prince of this World. The attitude of the zaddikim, as reflected in their tales, is quite different. Whether the world is good or evil depends on our relationship to it. When Rabbi Pinhas heard of the great misery among the needy, he listened, sunk in grief, then cried, "Let us draw God into the world, and all need will be quenched." "My holiness, which is the world, depends upon your holiness," the Maggid of Zlotchov expounded the injunction to be holy. "As you sanctify my name below, so is it sanctified in the heights of Heaven. For it is written:

'Give ye strength unto God.' '' Commenting on the Talmudic tale of a wise man versed in the lore of the stars who found the paths of the firmament as bright and clear as the streets of his native town, Rabbi Shalom Shakhna exclaimed, "If only we could say about ourselves that the streets of our city are as clear and bright to us as the paths of the firmament! For to let the hidden life of God shine out in this lowest world, the world of bodiliness, that is the greater feat of the two!" "The way in this world is like the edge of a blade," said Rabbi Moshe Leib of Sasov; "On this side is the netherworld and on that side is the netherworld, and the way of life lies in between."[12]

A Hasid of Rabbi Moshe of Kobryn, who was very poor, complained that his wretched circumstances were an obstacle to learning and praying. "In this day and age," said Rabbi Moshe, "the greatest devotion, greater than learning and praying, consists in accepting the world exactly as it happens to be." "I often hear men say: 'I want to throw up the world,' '' said the Rabbi of Ger. "But I ask you: Is the world yours to throw up?" "The other nations too believe that there are two worlds," said Rabbi Hanokh of Alexander. "They too say: 'In the other world.' The difference is this: They think that the two are separate and severed, but Israel professes that the two worlds are essentially one and shall, indeed, become one."[13] "Man was created for the purpose of unifying the two worlds," comments Buber. "He contributes toward this unity by holy living, in relationship to the world in which he has been set, at the place on which he stands."

> God's grace consists precisely in this, that He wants to let Himself be won by man, that He places Himself, so to speak, into man's hands. God wants to come to His world, but He wants to come to it through man. This is the mystery of our existence, the super-human chance of mankind.[14]

How then should we live in this world that it is given us to hallow? A little child and a thief can teach of us the 10 principles of service, the Maggid of Mezritch said to Rabbi Zusya:

> "From the child you can learn three things:
>> He is merry for no particular reason;
>> Never for a moment is he idle;

> When he needs something, he demands it vigorously.
> The thief can instruct you in seven things:
>> He does his service by night;
>> If he does not finish what he has set out to do in one
>> night, he devotes the next night to it;
>> He and those who work with him, love one another;
>> He risks his life for slight gains;
>> What he takes has so little value for him, that he
>> gives it up for a very small coin;
>> He endures blows and hardship, and it matters
>> nothing to him;
>> He likes his trade and would not exchange it for any
>> other."[15]

Although you should demand vigorously what you need, you should still practice the *wei-wu-wei,* or action of the whole being of Taoism which informs the second part of Buber's classic *I and Thou.* Such action appears like non-doing because it does not intervene or interfere but flows with things. "What you pursue, you don't get," Rabbi Pinhas used to say. "But what you allow to grow slowly in its own way, comes to you. Cut open a big fish, and in its belly you will find the little fish lying head down." The big fish stays still, and the little fish swims into its mouth.

By far the largest number of Hasidic tales on prayer center on *kavana,* the intention one brings to one's prayers. We have already seen the importance for some of the zaddikim of the distinction between *kavana*—the dedication of one's whole being—and *kavanot,* the magical mystical intentions that, following the prayerbook of Rabbi Isaac Luria, one consciously brings to one's actions and prayers. The Maggid of Mezritch himself, although founder of that line of Hasidism that emphasized the nullification of the concrete, praised the "Strong Thief" of *kavana* over the knowledge of *kavanot:*

> Every lock has its key which is fitted to it and opens it. But there are strong thieves who know how to open without keys. They break the lock. So every mystery in the world can be unriddled by the particular kind of meditation fitted to it. But God loves the thief who breaks the lock open: I mean the man who breaks his heart for God.[16]

The disciples of Rabbi Pinhas complained to him that since they were using the prayer book of Isaac Luria for their prayers, they had lost the sense of intensified life which prayer had always given them. "You have put all the strength and purposefulness of your thinking into the *kavanot* of the holy names, and the combinations of the letters," Rabbi Pinhas told them, "and have deviated from the essential: to make your hearts whole and dedicate them to God." Rabbi Zevi Hirsh of Rymanov once complained to his teacher that whenever he prayed he saw fiery letters and words flash before his eyes. Menahem Mendel was surprised that this bothered him, since these were the mystical concentrations of Isaac Luria. "I want to pray concentrating only on the meaning of the words," Rabbi Hirsh explained. "What you have in mind," said Rabbi Mendel, "is a very high rung which only one man in a whole generation can reach: that of having learned all secret wisdom and then praying like a little child."[17]

Kavana means bringing one's whole soul and life into prayer, and the zaddikim took this quite literally, even to the point of being prepared to die in prayer. When someone asked Rabbi Shlomo of Karlin to promise to visit him the next day, Rabbi Shlomo protested that when he said the evening and morning prayer, his soul went out to the very rim of life. "Perhaps I shall not die this time either, but how can I now promise to do something at a time after the prayer?"

Every morning before going to prayer, Rabbi Uri of Strelisk saw to his house and said his last goodbye to his wife and children. Rabbi Mordecai of Lekhovitz taught that the essence of prayer is that at the moment of saying "Lord" one must only think of offering oneself up to the Lord, so that even if one's soul should leave one with the "Lord," and one were not able to add the word "world," it would be enough for one. Similarly, his disciple Rabbi Moshe of Kobryn taught that one should give to God all the strength that is in one in the very first word of prayer, so that God must give him an abundance of new strength if he is to go on with the prayer. He also taught that when one utters a word before God, he must enter into that word with every one of his limbs. "How can a big human being possibly enter into a little word?" asked one of his listeners. "Anyone who thinks himself bigger than the word," replied the zaddik, "is not the kind of person we are talking about."[18]

A favorite target of the zaddik's criticism was prayer without *kavana*. The Baal Shem once refused to enter a House of Prayer because it was "crowded with teachings and prayers from wall to wall and from floor to ceiling," and the words did not come from hearts lifted to heaven.

Rabbi Levi Yitzhak once asked a reader why he had grown hoarse. "Because I prayed before the pulpit," answered the reader. "Quite right," said Levi Yitzhak. "If one prays before the pulpit one grows hoarse, but if one prays before the living God, then one does not grow hoarse."

Once after he had recited the Eighteen Benedictions, the Rabbi of Berditchev greeted several members of the congregation as though they had come back from a long journey. "Why are you so astonished?" he said. "You were far away, weren't you? You in a marketplace, and you on a ship with a cargo of grain." On the other hand, when he criticized some young men for rattling off their prayers, they pointed out that the mother can understand the babbling sounds of the child that all the scholars and sages of the world cannot.[19]

To the great zaddikim it was possible to bring true prayer and *kavana* into the very midst of worldliness. The Baal Shem told of a man so hounded by his business that he almost forgets there is a Maker of the world. But when the time for the Afternoon Prayer comes, he heaves a sigh of regret that he has spent his day on idle matters, runs into a bystreet and prays. "God holds him dear, very dear and his prayer pierces the firmament."

Whenever Pearl, the wife of Levi Yitzhak of Berditchev, kneaded and baked the loaves of bread for the sabbath, she prayed: "Lord of the world, I beg you to help me that, when my husband Levi Yitzhak says the blessing upon these loaves on the Sabbath, he may have in his mind what I have in my mind this very hour that I knead them and bake them."

When some opponents complained at how the Hasidim prayed after the hour set for prayer had passed and then sat down together and drank schnapps, Rabbi Israel of Rizhyn explained to them that this is really a counter-ruse against the Evil Urge who torments those who pray with alien thoughts. After prayer the Hasidim tell one another what is burdening their hearts and wish that God may grant them their desire. "And since—so our sages say— prayers can be said in any language whatsoever, this speaking and answering of theirs while drinking is also regarded as prayer. But all the Evil Urge sees is that they are eating and drinking and using everyday speech, and so he stops bothering his head about them." Once the Evil Urge came to Rabbi Mikhal of Zlotchov while he was praying. "Go away," he said to it, "and come back when I am eating. While one is praying, there must be no arguments."[20]

Kavana is deeper than any conscious will or intention. When Rabbi Bunam's enemies asked him why he delayed praying every morning, he replied, "One must wait to pray until all one's bones are awake." It is not our conscious intentions but our basic attitudes that are essential.

Asked what constitutes a true Jew, Rabbi Menahem Mendel of Vorki replied, "Upright kneeling, silent screaming, motionless dance."[21] Here I must repeat what Rabbi Uri of Strelisk said of prayer, because it is relevant, but also because it moves me so deeply:

> We know very well how we ought to pray, and still we cry for help in the need of the moment. The soul wishes us to cry out in spiritual need, but we are not able to express what the soul needs. And so we pray that God may accept our call for help, but also that he, who knows that which is hidden, may hear the silent cry of the soul.[22]

"Believe me," Rabbi Barukh said to his grandson, concerning prayer, "a single true gesture, even if it be only that of the small toe, is enough."

Once a villager brought his dull-witted son with him on the Day of Atonement to be sure the boy did not eat something without knowing better. The boy wanted to blow his whistle, but the father kept his hand on his pocket until the Closing Prayer, when the boy snatched at his pocket, took out the whistle, and blew a loud note. All the congregants were frightened and confused, but the Baal Shem later testified that the boy had made things easy for him. The retarded boy's whistling was "a single true gesture."

"Before I was in the Land of Israel," said R. Menahem Mendel of Vitebsk, "all my thoughts and desires were intent on saying a prayer just once in exactly the right way. But since I am in this land, all I want is just once to say 'Amen' in the right way."

Levi Yitzhak was so intent on saying "one" when counting the atoning drops of blood that he fell on the floor and lay as one dead. When he revived toward evening, he rushed up to the pulpit, shouting: ". . . and one!" Then he came to, and said the prayers in the correct sequence.[23]

Rabbi Zusya's mother did not pray from the book because she could not read. "But wherever she said the blessing in the morning, in that place the radiance of the Divine Presence rested the livelong day." Once when Zusya was a guest in the house of the Rabbi of Neskhizh, the host heard sounds after midnight, and listening, heard Zusya running back and forth, saying, "Lord of the world, I love you! But what is there for me to do?" The Rabbi of Neskhizh then grew frightened to hear the sound of whistling. Zusya had recalled that he knew how to whistle, and whistled a tune for God.

Once Levi Yitzhak delayed reciting the "All Vows" (the *Kol Nidre* prayer) on the Day of Atonement until a woman who came every year had arrived. When the woman became aware of this, she was filled with great joy and said to God: "Lord of the world, what shall I wish you in return for the good you have vouchsafed me! I wish you may have as much joy of your children as you have just now granted me!" Then, even while she was speaking, an hour replete with the grace of God came upon the world.[24]

6

Overcoming Dualism

The Hasidic demand that we discover and perform our own created task, that we channel the passion of the "evil" urge into the realization of our personal uniqueness, that we act and love with *kavana,* or inner intention, implies the strongest possible rejection of all those ways whereby we divide our lives into airtight compartments and escape becoming whole. Becoming whole does not mean "spiritual" wholeness, or the wholeness of the individuated Self within the unconscious (to use the language of Jung). It means that personal wholeness the necessary corollary of which is the wholeness of our lives. Our true wholeness is not the perfection of our "immortal soul" but the fulfillment of our created task. Only the latter brings our personal uniqueness into being in integral relation with the creation over against which we are set. Our existence does not take place *within* ourselves but in *relationship* to what is *not* ourselves. To make our goal spiritual perfection, consequently, means a foreshortening of our personal existence.

The Rabbi of Kotzk, we have seen, explained the biblical injunction, "Ye shall be holy unto me," as the demand not for perfection, but for authentic humanity: "You shall be holy unto me, but as men. You shall be humanly holy unto me." We are not asked to be saints, or superhuman, but to be holy in the measure and manner of the human, in the measure and manner of our personal resources. This is a seemingly easier demand than perfection, but in fact it is harder; for it asks you to do what you really *can* do, rather than despair over what you cannot.

To open our lives to the holy does not mean to rise above our situation. It means to bring our situation into dialogue with God. The openness to the holy does not mean leaving the everyday for a higher spiritual sphere, but "hallowing the everyday" through a genuine openness to what meets you. "Whoever says that the words of the Torah are one thing and the words of the world another," said Rabbi Pinhas of Koretz, "must be regarded as a man who denies God."

C. H. Dodd, the biblical scholar, said, "Many people seem to think that everything that happened in the Bible happened on Sunday." If there ought be no dualism of "sacred" words and "secular" words, neither ought there to be a dualism between words and silence. When the Yehudi discovered that a young man had taken a vow of silence for 3 years except for the Torah and prayer, he called the young man to him and asked him why it was that he did not see a single word of his in the world of truth. When the young man justified his silence by talking of the "vanity of speech," the Yehudi warned him that he who only learns and prays is murdering the world of his own soul. "What do you mean by the 'vanity of speech'?" continued the Yehudi, almost in the language of Lao-Tzu. "Whatever you have to say can be vanity, or it can be truth."

The Rabbi of Rizhyn imposed upon a confirmed sinner a terrible penance: "From now until you die, you shall not utter a single word of prayer with empty lips; but you shall preserve the fullness of every word." The sinner himself had brought the rabbi the list of his sins to have penance imposed on him. The rabbi's response not only demanded a sincere inner repentance, but a wholehearted *turning* of his existence.

"Man is like a tree," said Rabbi Uri of Strelisk. "If you stand in front of a tree and watch it incessantly to see how it grows and to see how much it is growing, you will see nothing at all. But tend it at all times, prune the runners, and keep the vermin from it and, all in good time, it will come into its growth." "It is the same with man," he added. "All that is necessary is for him to overcome his obstacles and he will thrive and grow. But it is not right to examine him every hour to see how much has been added to his growth."

If there is any single evil in our culture which overtops all others, it is this one of examining and measuring people all the time to see how far along they have come in school, in training, in business and professional life, in maturity, in self-realization, in comparison with their brothers and sisters, their classmates, their colleagues and fellow workers, or their neighbors. Even our "spiritual life" comes fully equipped, like Benjamin Franklin's chart of virtues, with measuring rods to show whether we have learned "receptive listening," realized our potential, grown in Christian humility and the love of God, or advanced in mystical contemplation or saintly perfection.

The more we try to discover how far along we are and what progress we have made, the more we will get in our own way. The only true growth is that which comes through spontaneity, through a response so great and wholehearted that we forget to be concerned about ourselves. A great violinist may negotiate for what he is to be paid for a concert, but each time he draws the bow over the strings, he does not think of how much money he is making.

Rabbi Hayyim of Krosno became so absorbed in watching a rope-dancer that his disciples asked him what it was that riveted his gaze to this foolish performance.

> "This man," he said, "is risking his life, and I cannot say why. But I am quite sure that while he is walking the rope, he is not thinking of the fact that he is earning a hundred gulden by what he is doing, for if he did, he would fall."[1]

Nothing could be more important for us contemporaries than the Hasidic emphasis on overcoming dualism—in prayer and in life, for the Hasidim admitted no final division between the two. In the title essay of *Hasidism and Modern Man,* Buber asserted that the kernel of Hasidic life is given over to decay and destruction—a judgment which could not please the very active movements of Satmar and Lubavitcher Hasidim that can be found in

America and Israel. But Buber held that Hasidism is still capable of working on the life of the present-day West, because of its central concern, preserved in personal as well as in communal existence, to overcome the fundamental separation between the sacred and the profane.

Although Kierkegaard and Marx already pointed to the crisis and alienation of modern man a century ago, and the psychoanalysts did the same at the turn of the century, only now can we really understand this crisis in its true depth and take the injured wholeness of the human upon us. We no longer know the holy face to face, but we know its heir, the "spiritual": We "recognize" it without allowing it to determine our life in any way. We take culture and ideas with grim seriousness: We place them on golden thrones to which their limbs are chained; but any claim of the spirit on personal existence is warded off through a comprehensive apparatus. "No false piety has ever attained this concentrated degree of inauthenticity."

To this behavior of present-day man who has got rid of the command of hallowing, "Hasidism sets the simple truth that the wretchedness of our world is grounded in its resistance to the entrance of the holy into lived life." "A life that does not seek to realize what the living person, in the ground of his self-awareness, understands or glimpses as the right is not merely unworthy of the spirit; it is also unworthy of life."[2] What underlay this seemingly harsh judgment was Buber's recognition that what was in question was not some separate sphere of the religious or holy, but the quality of life itself, its call to become "humanly holy" in the measure and manner of our personal existence.

Nothing could be a clearer judgment on the dualism between the "religious" and the everyday than the comment Rabbi Pinhas made to the assembled congregation when they recited the Psalms in noisy confusion on the eve of the Day of Atonement, before the *Kol Nidre* prayer:

> Why do you exert yourselves so much? Probably because you feel that your words are not mounting upward. And why not? Because you have told nothing but lies the entire year. He who lies throughout the year, gets a lying tongue. And how can a lying tongue shape true words which mount to Heaven? I, who am talking to

you, know all about it, because I myself had a hard time with this matter. So you can believe me: You must assume the burden of not telling lies. Then you will get a truthful tongue, and the words it shapes will fly to God.[3]

Schneur Zalman, we will recall, asked his son with what he prayed and was answered by a biblical verse belonging to the "spiritual" sphere. But when his son asked his father the same question, the *rav* answered, "I pray with the floor and the bench"—the indispensable elements of the everyday world that sustained him in the midst of prayer as in his other activities.[4] He did not have to leave the world to pray. On the contrary, it was only because he was firmly grounded in the world, the everyday world, that he could pray.

Let us look more fully at the story of "Penance" that we mentioned briefly above. A confirmed sinner who allowed no evil urge to pass him by came to an older rabbi, handed him a list of all the sins he had ever committed, and asked to have a penance imposed on him. The older rabbi sent him to Rabbi Israel of Rizhyn who was young enough to take such a burden on himself. After Rabbi Israel had read the whole list carefully, he imposed on the sinner this penance: "No matter what word of prayer you utter, from now until you die, you shall not utter a single word of prayer with empty lips; but you shall preserve the fullness of every word."[5]

I called this "a terrible penance" because the rabbi's response demanded not just a sincere inner repentance but a wholehearted turning of his existence. Only thus could a person who was used to living moment by moment in falsehood and inner division bring the whole of his life and intention into prayer and thus preserve the fullness of every word. What the sinner hoped for, instead, was a "penance" that would shrive him of guilt and allow him to continue living exactly as he had been before. This crystallized dualism was no longer open to him as a way, once the Rabbi of Rizhyn had given him a true response to his question.

In a way we are all like this sinner on whom the terrible penance was imposed. Each of us shuns the awful task of sustaining the life of prayer by bringing ourselves with all that we know and have been to each situation.

My chief advisor for my dissertation—Professor Arnold Bergstraesser—demanded of me when I had finished it, "What will keep you from reading this dissertation in 10 years and asking yourself, 'Did I know that then!'?" What he meant, I have realized ever more deeply in the more than thrice 10 years since, was that all the marvelous thoughts that I had gleaned from my study of Buber's thought might become lost, closed over, as the waters close over the deep. Not because the insights were untrue, but because I might fail to authenticate them and make them real by bringing them into my life.

Our age is dominated, perhaps more than any before, by a dualism in which people live in one world and have their ideals and symbols in another. Our alternatives seem increasingly to be reality divested of symbols, or symbols divested of reality. It is we who decide on each new battlefield whether the prevailing direction of religion and our lives is toward a dualism in which the spirit has no binding claim upon life, and life falls apart into unhallowed segments, or toward the continual overcoming of that dualism by taking up again and again the task of hallowing the creation that has been given to us. Every rung of human existence can be a ground of hallowing if we put off the habitual. We can overcome this dualism by the insistence, in each human and social sphere anew, that the spirit be relevant to life and that life be open to the demand of the spirit. We meet God not in the structures of the theologians and the concepts of the philosophers, but in the events and meetings of concrete life.

PART III

The Bond between Spirit and Spirit

7

Teaching and Learning

*I*n a sense, everything that we have considered in the preceding chapters has to do with teaching and learning, since the zaddik by his every action teaches his Hasidim to live a more human way of life. In this chapter, however, we are concerned not with *what* the zaddik teaches, and the Hasid learns, but with *how*. By "how" I do not mean a technique that may be applied across the board, ignoring the uniqueness of the person taught and of the relation between zaddik and Hasid. I mean rather an approach, a mode that informs Hasidic teaching and learning. This approach or mode differs from zaddik to zaddik. Indeed, each zaddik had a unique approach to teaching, and even that varied from Hasid to Hasid and situation to situation.

The most important "how" we have already pointed to in Chapter 2, namely, telling a story or tale as opposed to discussing concepts. Often, as we have seen, there is even a story within a story, a tale within a tale. Here we can go beyond and look at the approach or mode implicit in the tale. In his Preface to *The Early Masters*, Buber points to a species of tale which he designates as "Teaching in Answer." In addition, the *Tales* includes some longer teachings and sermons.

But not a single passage hails from the extensive theoretical writings of Hasidism; all are taken from the popular literature, where they supplement what is told of the lives of the zaddikim. All this has an entirely oral character, not a literary one.[1]

In his Introduction to *The Early Masters,* Buber stresses again that the zaddik, the helper for both body and soul, earthly and heavenly matters, teaches and guides in conducting one's affairs and remaining steadfast beneath the blows of destiny, but only until one is able to venture on alone.

He does not relieve you of doing what you have grown strong enough to do for yourself. He does not lighten your soul of the struggle it must wage in order to accomplish its particular task in this work. And all this also holds for the communication of the soul with God. The zaddik must make communication with God easier for his hasidim, but he cannot take their place.[2]

It is not surprising that Buber sees the relation between teacher and taught as one of true dialogue. The teacher helps his disciples find themselves, but in hours of desolation it is the disciples who help their teacher find *himself* again.

The teacher kindles the souls of his disciples and they surround him and light his life with the flame he has kindled. The disciple asks, and by his manner of asking unconsciously evokes a reply, which his teacher's spirit would not have produced without the stimulus of the question.[3]

I was startled when I reread that last sentence for the first time in a great many years; for it states explicitly what I myself learned from my own dialogue with Martin Buber. Once after an incredibly strenuous and exhausting two days as visiting lecturer at a college, I recalled Buber's statement to me, "I wish people would ask me more real questions," and I understood it with a depth I had never previously attained. Buber was not saying that he was a fount of knowledge, but that if persons approached him with *real* questions, then something would come into being between him and them that would not otherwise have arisen.

"Why is the Feast of Revelation designated as the time we

were given the Torah rather than the time we received the Torah?" one Hasid asked the zaddik. "The giving took place on the day commemorated by this feast," the rabbi replied, "but the receiving takes place at all times. It was given to all equally, but they did not all receive in equal measure." This same dialogical understanding of teaching, or Torah, is conveyed in a Hasidic commentary on the verse, "And these words which I command thee this day, shall be upon thy heart." "The verse does not say 'in thy heart,' " the zaddik pointed out. "For there are times when the heart is shut. But the words lie upon the heart, and when the heart opens in holy hours, they sink deep down into it."[4]

In his Introduction, Buber gives us an important hint about the "how" of Hasidic teaching by contrasting eras such as ours, when the world of the spirit is on the decline with epochs of flowering, such as that of the first three generations of the Hasidim. Only in the former is teaching, even on its highest level, regarded as a profession.

> In epochs of flowering, disciples live with their master just as apprentices in a trade lived with theirs, and "learn" by being in his presence, learn many things for their work and their life both because he wills it, or without any willing on his part.[5]

This means that what is essential for this sort of teaching is not any "institution of higher learning," even the finest, but genuine community.

Knowledge as an objective body of information that can be acquired and mastered is treated disparagingly by the zaddikim, even though many of them were great Talmudic scholars themselves. The Baal Shem said: "When I reach a high rung of knowledge, I know that not a single letter of the teachings is within me, and that I have not taken a single step in the service of God." One of the longest of the tales tells of a learned man from Lithuania who used to interrupt the sermons of Levi Yitzhak of Berditchev with hair-splitting arguments. Hearing that Rabbi Barukh of Mezbizh said, "If he comes to me he will not be able to say anything at all," the learned man went to him, only to discover that he had forgotten everything and had become an ignorant man.

When the Maggid of Mezritch expounded a passage of the

kabbala before the Baal Shem, the Baal Shem said, "You have expounded correctly, but you have not true knowledge, because there is no soul in what you know." A similar event took place a generation later. In his youth, Rabbi Israel of Koznitz studied 800 books of the kabbala, but the first time he saw the Maggid of Mezritch face to face, he instantly knew that he knew nothing at all.[6]

We shall not be surprised after this to learn that the zaddikim did not equate truth with knowledge. Rabbi Pinhas of Koretz told his disciples that he had found nothing more difficult than to overcome lying. "I broke every bone I had, and at last I found a way out." Truth here is truth in one's living, not in what one knows. "For the sake of truth, I served twenty-one years," Rabbi Pinhas said. "Seven years to find out what truth is, seven to drive out falsehood, and seven to absorb truth."

A story of Rabbi Zusya shows this same attitude toward truth. Zusya was the only disciple of the Great Maggid who did not transmit the teachings in his name, for the simple reason that he never heard his sermons to the end. No sooner did the Maggid begin to recite a verse, than Zusya was overcome with ecstasy, screaming and gesticulating so wildly that he had to be taken out. Rabbi Israel of Rizhyn, who told this story, commented: "If a man speaks in the spirit of truth and listens in the spirit of truth, one word is enough, for with one word can the world be uplifted, and with one word can the world be redeemed."[7]

Essential to Hasidism, as to Zen, is the conviction that true learning and teaching take place, not out of books, but out of the living chain between the teacher and the taught, between generation and generation. Rabbi Barukh of Mezbizh said that one can only understand the words of a Talmudic master by linking one's own soul to the soul of the master. Only then will one learn the true meaning of his words. One must in turn do the same with the other masters. Only thus can one live with the uniqueness of each master and do justice to both. This is a profoundly dialogical process: When a word is spoken in the name of its speaker, the latter's lips move in the grave, and the lips of the person who utters the word move like those of the dead master. That is why Rabbi Mordecai of Lekhovitz, one of the later masters, told his disciples that the zaddik cannot say any words of the teachings

unless he first links his soul to the soul of his dead teacher or to
that of his teacher's teacher. Only then is link joined to link and
the chain of the generations formed from Moses to the present.

Rabbi Mordecai of Nezkhizn, who rarely spoke words of
teaching and then only a few, explained his restraint: "One must
unite with the angel-prince of the Torah in order to receive in
one's heart the word of teaching. Only then does what one says
enter the heart of one's hearers so that each receives what he
requires for his own particular needs."[8] With this we are back to
the unique.

When a disciple begged Rabbi Shmelke of Nikolsburg to teach
him how to prepare his soul for the service of God, he sent him
to see the way Rabbi Abraham Hayyim, who at that time was
still an innkeeper, cleaned the dishes so that not the slightest trace
of food was left, and cleaned and dried the pots and pans so that
they did not rust. When Shneur Zalman of Ladi was asked by a
gendarme why God needed to ask Adam "Where art thou?" the
rav replied in terms of the unique situation of the gendarme—
"You have lived forty-six years. How far along are you?"—calling
him to account and back into true dialogue. This too is teaching
and learning "from heart to heart." When Rabbi Yehudah Zevi
was asked to tell words of teaching that he had heard from his
teacher, Rabbi Uri of Strelisk, Yehudah Zevi replied: "The
teachings of my teacher are like manna that enters the body but
does not leave it." When his interlocutor continued to press him,
Rabbi Yehudah Zevi tore open the coat over his breast and cried:
"Look into my heart! There you will learn what my teacher is."[9]

Although teaching and learning are integrally linked in the
Hasidic tales, we can gain something by speaking separately of
ways of teaching and ways of learning. This is particularly so when
teaching and learning take place without conscious intention on
the part of teacher or learner. When the Baal Shem in the midst
of praying said to God, "Whatever is in me, everything, new and
old, for you alone," his disciples protested, "But the rabbi tells
words of teaching to *us* too!" "As when the barrel overflows,"
the Baal Shem replied. The Maggid of Mezritch distinguished between two types of zaddikim: one who spent their time on mankind, teaching them and taking trouble about them, and the other
who concerned themselves only with studying the teachings. "The

first bear nourishing fruit, like the date palm; the second are like the cedar: lofty and unfruitful."[10]

Both the Baal Shem and the Maggid of Mezritch were fond of the simile of how the father teaches the child to walk by moving away from it and then allowing it to come up close again. One form of Hasidic teaching, as we have seen, is that of direct presence, which sometimes expresses itself only in silence and taking someone to one's heart. Rabbi Mordecai of Lechovitz testified that he learned how to convert persons through the way Rabbi Aaron of Karlin dealt with him when he was a child. When little Mordecai's father complained that he did not persevere in his studies, Rabbi Aaron told the father to leave him alone with the child. Then he lay down and took the child to his heart, holding him silently until the father returned, at which time he said, "I have given him a good talking-to. From now on, he will not be lacking in perseverance."

Sometimes, however, Hasidic teaching takes the form that Viktor Frankl might call "paradoxical intention." Once Yehiel Mikhal sought out the Baal Shem while he was quite young and still uncertain whether he wanted to be his disciple. The Baal Shem took him on a journey. When it was evident that they had lost their way, Mikhal exclaimed, "Why, Rabbi! Have you lost your way?" "God has fulfilled your desire to have a chance to laugh at me," the Baal Shem replied. These words pierced young Mikhal's heart, and without further argument he joined the master with his whole soul.[11]

An interesting variant of this theme is the story of the disciple of Barukh of Mezbizh, whose thinking penetrated so far into the nature of God that he became entangled in doubts. Rabbi Barukh went to visit him and said, "I know what is hidden in your heart.

> You have passed through the fifty gates of reason. You begin with a question and think and think up and answer—and the first gate opens, and to a new question! And again you plumb it, find the solution, fling open the second gate—and look into a new question. On and on like this, deeper and deeper, until you have forced open the fiftieth gate. There you stare at a question whose answer no man has ever found, for if there were one who knew it, there would no longer be freedom of choice. But if you dare to probe still further, you plunge into the abyss."

"So I should go back all the way, to the very beginning?" cried the disciple.

"If you turn, you will not be going back," said Rabbi Barukh. "You will be standing beyond the last gate: you will stand in faith."[12]

A very different mode of teaching is through reproach, reproof, and rebuff, though this too can be seen as a part of the father's teaching the child to walk through distancing himself. The Baal Shem once sent his disciple Rabbi Wolf Kitzes to visit a rich and hospitable man who lived in a nearby city. After the man had lavishly entertained Rabbi Wolf and presented him with a generous gift, he asked his guest, "Don't you think that this is the proper way to practice hospitality?" Rabbi Wolf only replied, "We shall see," after which the host had such a terrible dream that he begged to be taken to his master. The Baal Shem received him with a smile. "Would you like to know where all that hospitality of yours has gone to?" he asked. "It has all gone into a dog's mouth." At this the rich man's heart awoke and turned to God, and the Baal Shem instructed him how to lift up his soul.[13]

The Maggid of Mezritch taught the two brothers, Shmelke and Pinhas, how to conduct themselves throughout the day, confirming and modifying all their habits as though he knew the whole of their lives. But in closing he said:

And before you lie down at night, you add up everything you have done during the day. And when a man calculates his hours and sees that he has not wasted a moment in idleness, when his heart beats high with pride, then—up in Heaven—they take all his good works, crush them into a ball, and hurl it down into the abyss.[14]

We will recall how the Seer of Lublin told the man who kept pestering him as to what to do about "alien thoughts," that to the person with holy thoughts an impure thought is "alien." "But you—you have just your own usual thoughts. To whom do you want to ascribe them?" The Seer had a disciple who fasted from Sabbath to Sabbath, which in the Jewish tradition meant taking neither food nor water. An hour before the end of the week, the disciple thought he would die if he did not take a drink of water. When he reached into the well for a drink, he thought, "A whole week's work wasted!'' This thought helped him overcome the temptation, but overcoming the temptation made him feel pride. When he became aware of this, he decided to make himself drink after all. Somehow he overcame this temptation too and finished the week without breaking his fast. When he crossed the Seer's threshold, the Seer, as we have seen, came out to greet him not with congratulations but with the word, "Patchwork!"[15] In this "cruel" way he taught him the difference between a work done all of a piece and a "spiritual achievement" that is of no value because it is not done with the whole soul.

A similar teaching through reproof is found in the story of *The Obliging Dream.* A man who pursued honors twice came to Rabbi Bunam and reported a dream in which his father announced to him that he was destined to be a leader. "I see," said Rabbi Bunam, "that you are prepared to become a leader of men." "If your father appears to you again," he added, "answer him that you are ready to lead, but that now he should also appear to the people whom you are supposed to lead."[16]

There are two Hasidic tales in which a zaddik refuses to learn from a dead rabbi, not even the Baal Shem Tov. "When learning from a rabbi, the disciple must resemble his teacher at least in one thing—in having a garment of flesh," said Rabbi Hayyim Meir Yehiel of Mogielnica. When the Yehudi appeared to Menahem Mendel of Kotzk in a dream and offered to teach him, Menahem Mendel said, "I do not want a teacher from the other world." In exact contrast, when Rabbi Bunam's son asks who will teach him after the death of his father, Bunam's disciple Yitzhak of Vorki says to him, "Take courage. Up to now he has taught you in his coat; from now on, he will teach you without his coat on."[17]

There is also a hint of how *not* to teach. One Sabbath a learned man asked Rabbi Barukh of Mezbizh for words of teaching because he spoke so well. "Rather than speak so well," said the grandson of the Baal Shem, "I should be stricken dumb."[18]

One way of learning that we have already seen is that of linking one's soul to one's teacher. Another has to do with the wisdom that is attained in the "between stage." The Maggid of Mezritch said that nothing in the world can change from one reality into another unless it first turns into nothing. Only through this reality of the between stage can one attain to wisdom, that is, to a thought which cannot be made manifest.

One may also learn through nature. After the Great Maggid's death, Schneur Zalman asked his fellow disciples, "Do you know why our master went to the pond every day at dawn and stayed there for a little while before coming home again? He was learning the song with which the frogs praise God. It takes a very long time to learn that song."

Rabbi Yehiel Mikhal stressed that one learns not only from one's teacher but from every person. "Even from one who is ignorant, or from one who is wicked, you can gain understanding as to how to conduct your life."[19]

As Buber stressed at the outset, the ultimate purpose of teaching is to enable the learner to find his or her own ground. "Often when someone comes to ask my advice, I hear him giving himself the answer to his question," said Rabbi Pinhas of Koretz. Rabbi Yehudah Zevi of Stretyn advised persons who have grown aware of a new way in which to serve God to carry it around with them secretly for 9 months, as though they were pregnant, and only at the end of that time to let others know of it.[20] This is a most important teaching in holding one's ground; for all too often persons imagine they have to trot out new insights and paths for the inspection of all their friends before they are justified in taking them seriously. It is as if we cannot accept our unique way unless we are confirmed by others in advance.

I cannot resist concluding this chapter with a modern comment on Hasidic teaching by my friend Elie Wiesel, especially since Elie takes the tale from a Zen Buddhist source and recasts it in the context of the enigmatic and troubling final 20 years of seclusion of the Kotzker rebbe. Asked in an interview about teaching children and adults, Wiesel said that he taught both the same way: teaching them to ask the right questions. When he came home from heder and then from the yeshivah, the lower and higher schools for Jewish children studying Hebrew, the Bible, and the Talmud, Wiesel's parents never asked him, "Did you give a good answer?" but always instead, "Did you ask a good question today?" This, to Wiesel, is the heart of Hasidic teaching (and that of Judaism in general), and he illustrates by telling the following story, which he adapts from Zen to Hasidism:

> Once upon a time a Hasid decided he had to know the meaning of truth. So he went looking in all kinds of schools. Nobody knew

the meaning of truth. Finally somebody told him, "There is a rebbe in Kotzk who knows everything. He knows the meaning of truth. Go to Kotzk." So our Hasid said goodbye to his friends, kissed his children, and began walking to Kotzk. After many months of wandering, he finally arrived in Kotzk. He asked a Hasid in the street, "Where is the rebbe's house?" He showed him. He came there. It was full of Hasidim. He asked, "Can I see the rebbe?" They laughed at him. Why did they laugh? Because the rebbe was known for his solitude. For twenty years he was alone. "You just came and you want to see him?" He said, "Yes. I have an important question to ask. I must see him." He could not get in.

But he was clever. He decided not to move from the anteroom and waited there until everybody was asleep. Then he opened the door and entered the rebbe's study. The rebbe looked up and demanded, "What do you want?" The Hasid said, "Rebbe, I came from very far. I have a very important question to ask." "What is the question?" "Rebbe, what is truth?" The rebbe looked at him and slapped his face. The Hasid began to cry. He said, "Rebbe, why did you slap my face? I am serious. I am sincere. I really want to know what is truth?" The rebbe again looked at him and again slapped his face. Then he opened the door and pushed the Hasid out. Our Hasid was very unhappy, you can imagine.

He left the rebbe's home and began walking. Then he saw an inn. He entered, sat at a table, and ordered a glass of wine, but he could not drink. He cried and cried. Suddenly an old Hasid came in. He said, "Brother, why do you cry?" "Leave me alone." "Brother, why do you cry?" So he explained: "I came to see the rebbe. I asked him a question, and he slapped my face twice." "Twice, do you say?" "Yes, twice." The old Hasid began pacing up and down, up and down, thinking, thinking. "Twice. You said twice." And suddenly he smiled. He stopped at the table and said, "You know, my dear friend, we in Kotzk have always believed that our rebbe is very wise. I did not know he was that wise!" Hearing that, our Hasid almost slapped *his* face. "Where is the wisdom in slapping my face?" He said, "Oh, you do not understand. If the rebbe slapped your face the first time, it was because he wanted to teach you something very important." "What is it?" "He wanted to teach you the importance of questions. If you have a question, idiot, why do you need an answer? Questions are better than answers. That is why he slapped your face the first time. But he slapped your face a second time because he wanted to teach you something even more important. He wanted to teach you actually that there is never any relationship between any question and any answer.''[21]

A year before he told the above story, Wiesel suggested a somewhat more comforting approach to Hasidic teaching as asking questions: ''A rebbe is not someone who gives the answers,'' Wiesel said. ''A rebbe is someone who shares his questions with you. But then, if they are articulated with enough sincerity, the questions become answers, or at least they become a beginning of an answer.''[22] No one can simply hand over the answers to us, but if we really hear the questions, take them into the depths of our souls, and make them our own, then our own answer may begin to take shape as a direction in which to move, a path to follow. This is the only meaningful human ''truth'' for which we can hope.

8

Love and Community

From *kavana* we can understand the unique approach of Hasidism to love and to helping one's fellow man. The Hasidim rejected emphatically the image of the helper who stands above the person he wants to help and reaches down a helping hand. "If you want to raise a man from mud and filth," said Rabbi Shlomo of Karlin, "you must go all the way down yourself, down into mud and filth. Then take hold of him with strong hands and pull him and yourself out into the light." This does not mean that you imitate his sins; but you must open yourself to the reality of the evil into which he has fallen and not try to bestow charity from above while keeping your soul free from any thing that might disturb it.

Rabbi Moshe Leib of Sasov learned to love when he went to an inn and heard one drunken peasant ask another, "Do you love me?" "Certainly I love you," replied the second. "I love you like a brother." But the first shook his head and insisted, "You don't love me. You don't know what I lack. You don't know what I need." The second peasant fell into sullen silence, but Rabbi Moshe Leib understood: "To know the need of men and to bear the burden of their sorrow, that is the true love of men." This love only exists in mutual relationship, in that dialogue in which one experiences the other's side of the relationship, knows the other from within. Each person needs to be loved, not in his universal humanity or divinity, but in his uniqueness, including what he lacks.

Rabbi Moshe Leib not only understood this; he lived it. He shared so earnestly in the spiritual and physical sufferings of others that their suffering became his own. When someone once expressed his astonishment at this capacity to share in another's troubles, he replied, "What do you mean 'share'? It is my own sorrow; how can I help but suffer it?"

The Yehudi, the "holy Jew," was asked why the stork is called devout or loving (*hasidah*) in the Talmud because he gives so much love to his mate and his young, but is classed in the Scriptures with the unclean birds. The Yehudi answered: "Because he gives love only to his own." We must love the other—the stranger, the enemy—even as we love our family. In both cases our love must be an openness and response to the unique person that we meet. Mixed with this insistence on concreteness is a good measure of Hasidic realism and humor, as in the story that the Rabbi of Zans used to tell about himself:

> In my youth when I was fired with the love of God, I thought I would convert the whole world to God. But soon I discovered that it would be quite enough to convert the people who lived in my town, and I tried for a long time, but did not succeed. Then I realized that my program was still much too ambitious, and I concentrated on the persons in my own household. But I could not convert them either. Finally it dawned on me: I must work upon myself, so that I may give true service to God. But I did not accomplish even this.[1]

The title of this tale is *Resignation*, resignation without any admixture of bitterness, despair, disillusionment, defeat. No other tale expresses so precisely my own history.

Like the novelist Irwin Shaw, author of *The Young Lions*, most people, including myriads of Jews, have accepted from the general culture the distorted understanding of the God of the "Old Testament" as a harsh and wrathful God in contrast to the loving and merciful God of the New. Hasidism not only stresses the love and mercy of God; it shows that to be a Hasid, a loyal follower of God, means to love one's fellowmen and even one's enemies.

It is a living embodiment of the dictum to "deal lovingly with thy neighbor as one like thyself." As such it demonstrates, as no amount of pointing to Leviticus can, that this injunction was taken over by Jesus from the Judaism in which he himself stood.

The love of Hasidism is not a spiritualized love, but a love involving the whole person. By the same token, it is not a purely forgiving love, but one that places a real demand upon the other—the demand of the relationship itself. The "hallowing of the everyday" means making the concrete relations of one's life essential, and real relationship includes both mutuality and passion. Mutuality means that love does not simply flow forth from the loving person to others; rather it moves back and forth within the dialogue between them as the fullest expression of that dialogue.

Rabbi Wolf of Zbarazh invited the coachman to come inside and get warm at a circumcision, and offered to take care of his horses while he did so. The coachman helped himself to glass after glass and stayed hour after hour. When the guests left at nightfall they found Rabbi Wolf standing beside the carriage, moving his arms and stamping his feet. When Rabbi Wolf rode in a carriage, he never permitted the whip to be used on the horses. "You do not even have to shout at them," he instructed the coachman. "You just have to know how to talk to them."

Once when Rabbi Zusya was traveling cross-country collecting money to ransom prisoners, he came on a room in an inn in which there was a large cage with all kinds of birds. Sensing how the birds wanted to fly through the spaces of the world again, Zusya opened the cage and freed these prisoners too. When the angry innkeeper returned and took him to task, Zusya cited the verse from the Psalms, "His tender mercies are over all His works." The innkeeper beat Zusya until his hand got tired and threw him out of the house, but Zusya went his way serenely. Zusya's whole life was a web of need and anguish, yet he accepted his suffering with such love that he did not recognize it as suffering.[2]

Hallowing the everyday and going out to meet the world with one's whole being meant, to the Hasidim, loving one's fellow. One midnight Rabbi Moshe Leib was disturbed in his study of the mystic teaching by the knock of a drunken peasant who asked to be let in and given a bed for the night. For a moment the zaddik's heart was full of anger at the "insolence" of this man who had no business in his house. But then he said silently in his heart: "And what business has he in God's world? But if God gets along with him, can I reject him?" He opened the door and prepared a bed. Moshe Leib used to visit all the sick boys in the town, sit at their bedside, and care for them. "He who is not willing to suck the pus from the sores of a child sick with the plague has not climbed even halfway up the mountain to the love of his fellowmen," he once said. When a learned but ungenerous man asked Rabbi Abraham of Stretyn for a drug to attain to the fear of God, Rabbi Abraham offered him instead one for the love of God. "That's even better!" cried the man. "Just you give it to me." "It is the love of one's fellowmen," replied the zaddik.[3]

When young Rabbi Eleazar of Koznitz was a guest in the house of Rabbi Naftali of Roptchitz, he expressed surprise at the drawn curtains before the windows: "If you want people to look in, then why the curtains? And if you do not want them to, why the window?" Rabbi Naftali asked him what explanation he would give. "When you want someone you love to look in," said Rabbi Eleazar, "you draw aside the curtain." After Rabbi Yehudah Zevi of Stretyn and Rabbi Shimon of Yaroslav had both dismounted from their carriages and greeted each other like brothers, Rabbi Yehudah Zevi remarked that he now understood the meaning of the popular saying: "Men can meet, but mountains never." "When one man considers himself just a human being, pure and simple, and the other does so too, they can meet. But if the one considers himself a lofty mountain, and other thinks the same, then they cannot meet."[4]

Not only teaching and learning, but all Hasidic life takes place within community, and community is both matrix and product of love. Even the most exalted zaddik is bound to the community. There is no room here for the lonely anchorite or hermit living in seclusion in the desert or the saint living on top of his pillar. "One of the great principles of Hasidism," writes Buber, "is that the zaddik and the people are dependent on one another." The zaddik guides not just through his teaching but also and even more through his day-by-day existence, "unemphatic, undeliberate, unconscious . . . the complete human being with his whole worldly life in which the completeness of the human being is tested. As a zaddik once said: 'I learned the Torah from all the limbs of my teacher.' " The zaddik helps and guides, but the disciples help the zaddik in his hours of desolation and light his life with the flame he has kindled. This reciprocal influence is given classic illustration in a tale of the Baal Shem which Buber entitles *The Strength of Community:*

> It is told:
> Once, on the evening after the Day of Atonement, the moon was hidden behind the clouds and the Baal Shem could not go out to say the Blessing of the New Moon. This weighed heavily on his spirit, for now, as often before, he felt that destiny too great to be gauged depended on the work of his lips. In vain he concentrated his intrinsic power on the light of the wandering star, to help it throw off the heavy sheath: whenever he sent some one out, he was told that the clouds had grown even more lowering. Finally he gave up hope.
> In the meantime, the Hasidim, who knew nothing of the Baal Shem's grief, had gathered in the front room of the house and begun to dance, for on this evening that was their way of celebrating with festal joy the atonement for the year, brought about by the zaddik's priestly service. When their holy delight mounted higher and higher, they invaded the Baal Shem's chamber, still dancing. Overwhelmed by their own frenzy of happiness, they took him by the hands, as he sat there sunk in gloom, and drew him into the round. At this moment, someone called outside. The night had suddenly grown light; in greater radiance than ever before, the moon curved on a flawless sky.[5]

This tale is immediately followed by *The Bird Nest,* which shows the strength of the community through a negative example. After the Baal Shem's disciples had dealt him "a painful separation" through going home while he was standing for a very long time praying in the House of Prayer, the Baal Shem told them the parable of a glorious many-colored bird that lighted atop a tall tree. The king of the country ordered a number of men to make themselves a human ladder, one standing on the shoulders of the other till they reached the top of the tree. It took a long time to build this living ladder; those nearest the ground lost patience and shook themselves free, and the ladder collapsed.

On the positive side, again, a tale is told of Rabbi Nahum of Tchernobil in which the humility of the Hasidism is matched by that of the zaddik; they go to him for help, but he at the same time looks to them for comfort. Going to the door, he sees them coming. "At this instant two arcs fused to a ring."

In the following generation, Rabbi Israel of Rizhyn speaks of the zaddikim as the letters, and the Hasidim who journey to them as the vowel signs. "The Hasidism need the zaddik, but he has just as much need of them. Through them he can be uplifted. Because of them he can sink—God forbid! They carry his voice, they sow his work in the world."[6]

Sometimes, of course, this reciprocity is shown in a tale, not of the zaddik and his Hasidim, but of the zaddik and a single Hasid:

> On a Friday, at the hour the zaddik examines his soul, the whole world grew dark for the Baal Shem, and the spark of life almost died within him. That was how one of his great disciples found him. "My master and teacher!" he said. His voice trembled and he could not utter another word. But even so he had caused new strength to flow into the Baal Shem's heart, and the flame of life grew strong within him.[7]

Only those with a calm soul can descend into the whirlpool of the souls they are helping, some of the early zaddikim warned. Indeed, there was a whole controversy around what the zaddik's relation should be to the "evil urge."[8] The extent to which it was a relationship from above to below also entailed the danger of an undue admiration that might go over into near worship. I devote Chapter 10 of my book, *The Human Way,* to "The Paradox of Religious Leadership." In this chapter I suggest that this phenomenon is *by its very nature* problematic, because the authentic religious leader who genuinely wants to lead his or her charges to greater immediacy in their dialogue with the divine tends to take the place of that immediacy by his or her very function as leader. The followers often foist upon the leader the task of vicariously representing them before God, even to the point of idolatry.[9]

Originally, Hasidic leadership devolved not so much on those who could receive a doctrine, but on those who could embody a way of life, bringing, as a result, the people to immediacy in relationship to God. Later, when hereditary dynasties of zaddikim arose, the rebbes lived in great palaces and were surrounded by awe and superstition so that the zaddik become almost a mediator between the people and God—the very opposite of his original function. "The zaddik, or rebbe, was not just a priest with a priestly function," I write in *The Human Way*, "but a leader responsible for the total life of his community and of each family and each individual in it. Therefore, his power for healing and help could equally easily become a power for domination and exploitation:

> Some zaddikim had sufficient wholeness that they could descend into the whirlpool. Others found themselves sucked down into the whirlpool. Still others were like the "wicked," of whom the Seer of Lublin spoke, who did not turn even on the threshold of hell; "for they thought they were being sent to hell to redeem the souls of others"! And some dark and enigmatic figures like Menahem Mendel of Kotzk abjured the task of leadership in the last years of their lives.[10]

Some zaddikim, like the Seer of Lublin, as he is portrayed in Martin Buber's great chronicle-novel *For the Sake of Heaven*, wished to hasten the coming of redemption through magical, mystical intentions and prayers, as a result of which their leadership is an essentially authoritarian one resting on that "miracle, mystery, and authority" that Dostoevsky's Grand Inquisitor espoused. Others, like the Seer's disciple, the holy Yehudi, as he is portrayed in *For the Sake of Heaven*, stayed clear of magic and taught that redemption can come only through our turning back to God with the whole of our individual and communal existence. The Yehudi's leadership rested, correspondingly, on the call to the turning that respects the power of response of every individual person.

> Through the Seer's emphasis on the divine power of the zaddik and through the awe of his disciples, the Seer holds the place of an oriental potentate in his congregation. The Yehudi, in contrast, preserves an informal and democratic relation with his disciples. The Seer uses his disciples for magic purposes; the Yehudi helps his disciples find the path they seek to pursue of and for themselves. He teaches his disciples that man's turning is not for the sake of individual salvation alone but for the redemption of the whole of creation—for the sake of the Shekinah, God's indwelling glory,

which is in exile. Redemption takes place not in isolation, moreover, but in a communal life of justice, love, and consecration.[11]

One-on-one, in Hasidism, is not always from the zaddik above to the Hasid below. Often it is simply from person to person on an equal level. This is suggested by a saying of Rabbi Pinhas of Koretz:

> When a man is singing and cannot lift his voice, and another comes and sings with him, another who can lift his voice, then the first will be able to lift his voice too. That is the secret of the bond between spirit and spirit.[12]

The title which Buber gives to this tale is not "The Helper," but "When Two Sing." Though one person can lift his voice and the other cannot, the true emphasis of the saying is on "the bond between spirit and spirit." This is shown equally clearly by the tale that follows it, "The Quickening," in which Rabbi Pinhas asserts that every human being has a light in Heaven, but that when two meet, the lights fuse, and a new light shines out of them.

No clearer expression could be found for Martin Buber's ontology of "the between." The angel born from this new light cannot live longer than 12 months unless those two beings meet on earth again before the time is up. If a rift appears in the carriage of the Divine Presence through one person hating and doing harm to another, Pinhas of Koretz also said, then it is up to us to fill it out by approaching our neighbor more closely than before. When someone expressed fear that he would crowd Rabbi Pinhas in his carriage, he said with affection, "Let us love each other more and we shall have a feeling of spaciousness," adding, "God is a greathearted friend."[13]

The mutuality of Hasidic life has never been expressed better than in Rabbi Yitzhak Eisik of Zhydatchov's saying, "The motto of life is 'Give and take.' Everyone must be both a giver and a receiver. He who is not both is as a barren tree." The person who tries to help others without receiving is like the famous "Giving Tree" in the children's story of that name which ends up a mere stump. That is because we do not exist fundamentally as role to role but as person to person. What we need from each other is not "solicitude" but love. Commenting on the verse in the Proverbs which reads, "As in water face answereth to face, so the heart of man to man," Rabbi Bunam said that only when the heart of one person leans down to the heart of its fellow will it see itself within her heart.

Once Rabbi Bunam and his Hasidim heard two porters in an inn interpret the weekly portion of the Torah in which Abraham made a covenant with Abimelech, the king of the Philistines. The reason that the text says, 'they two made a covenant,' one of the porters suggested, is that they did not become one but remained two.[14] That is how it is with every true person-to-person relation. This two-ness does not mean a focus on difference, and still less on that comparison of one with the other through which people seek false confirmation, feeling themselves better than others, or fall into false disconfirmation, imagining themselves worse. We each of us have our own ground on which to stand, and from which to go out to meet others. If we exist only in comparison with each other, then we are only consciousness plus social role, and not persons at all.

When Pinhas of Koretz talked of differences, he did not mean such comparison at all, but rather that uniqueness that constitutes the person, but also the community. No face is like any other because "every human being sucks the living strength of God from another place, and all together they make up Man." When Rabbi Rafael of Bershad was called on to give the decisive testimony in condemning a Jew accused of a crime who he knew was guilty, he struggled with himself in prayer until dawn and then lay down and died.

He was known far and wide for his integrity, so he would not perjure himself. But he preferred dying to bringing a fellow Jew into ignominy.

Another early master, Rabbi Yehiel Mikhal of Zlotchov, used to say before beginning to pray: "I join myself to all of Israel, to those who are more than I, that through them my thought may rise, and to those who are less than I, so that they may rise through my thought." Rabbi Mikhal interpreted Hillel's saying, "If I am not for myself, who will be for me? And if I am for myself, what am I" to mean that when I participate in the congregation, whatever any member of the congregation does in my place counts just as though I had done it myself. But if I do not participate in the congregation, "then everything in the way of good works which I have wrought alone is less than nothing in the eyes of God."[15]

Rabbi Hayyim of Zans, a later master, told his followers the story of two men who had lost their way in the forest. Asked the way out of the forest by the second man, the first said, "I don't know, but I can point out the ways that lead further into the thicket, and after that, let us find the way together." "So, my congregation," the rabbi concluded, "let us look for the way together."[16]

When the Kotzker rebbe in the days of his seclusion explained his withdrawing from men to his friend Rabbi Yitzhak of Vorki by interpreting "They that take for Me an offering" from the weekly portion of the Torah, his friend offered a directly opposite interpretation of the same verse:

> "When a Jew wishes to take the right way, God's way, he must take what every man has to offer him. He should accept the companionship of every man and by associating with every man receive from him whatever that man can give him for the way of God."[17]

A natural corollary of the Hasidic emphasis on community was the concern for social justice and for the poor and the refusal to pander to the rich. When the opponents of Rabbi Mikhal sent a rich man to find out why he delayed so long before beginning to pray, Mikhal asked him: "Is there no one more learned than you here, to put this question to me?"

> "Yes, indeed!" answered Perles. "There are men here, so learned, that I do not reach even to their ankles."
> "And why," said the zaddik, "don't they ask me?"
> "Well, the other replied, "they are poor, and they have broken hearts—as poor men have. But I am rich and my heart is sound."
> "Well, then," said the rabbi, "you yourself admit that the teachings do not ask me why I delay my prayer; only sixty thousand rubles are asking me. But sixty thousand rubles shall not have the pleasure of hearing me reveal why I delay my prayer."[18]

Rabbi Shmelke of Nikolsburg said: "The poor man gives the

rich man more than the rich gives the poor. More than the poor man needs the rich man, the rich is in need of the poor."

Once the Maggid of Koznitz was visited by a rich man who boasted that all he needed to eat was bread and salt and a drink of water. "What are you thinking of!" the rabbi reproved him. "You must eat roast meat and drink mead, like all rich people." After the disgruntled rich man had left, the maggid's disciples asked him the reason for this odd request. "Not until he eats meat," said the maggid, "will he realize that the poor man needs bread. As long as he himself eats bread, he will think the poor man can live on stones."

Once Rabbi Noftali of Roptchitz returned home weary after speaking in his sermon of the many needs of the poor for the coming Passover. When his wife asked him what his sermon accomplished, he replied, "half of what is necessary": "You see, the poor are now ready to take. As for the other half, whether the rich are ready to give—I don't know about that yet."[19]

When Rabbi Zev Wolf of Zbarazh's wife took a servant girl to the court of arbitration because she refused to replace a dish she was accused of breaking, Zev Wolf said he was coming too. His wife objected that this was not fitting and, besides, she knew very well what to say to the court. "You know it very well," the zaddik replied. "But the poor orphan, your servant, in whose behalf I am coming, does not know it, and who except me is there to defend her cause?"

When Levi Yitzhak discovered that the girls who kneaded the dough for the unleavened bread for Passover drudged from early morning until late at night, he cried aloud to the congregation: "Those who hate Israel accuse us of baking the unleavened bread with the blood of Christians. But no, we bake them with the blood of Jews!"[20]

Many zaddikim refused to keep money in the house overnight. Many were particularly concerned with helping the poor. After Rabbi Zev Wolf was robbed, he ran after the thieves and begged them to regard all they had taken as gifts from him, but warned them to be careful about a jug that had come in contact with a sick man. From this time on, every evening before he went to bed he declared all his possessions common property, so that thieves who might come again would not be guilty of theft. Rabbi

Mordecai of Neskhizh saved his money to buy a citron for the Feast of Tabernacles but gave it all away to a man whose horse had collapsed so he could buy another. "What does it matter?" Rabbi Mordecai said to himself. "Everybody will say the blessing over the citron; I shall say mine over this horse."[21]

Rabbi Shmelke of Nikolsburg, having no money in the house, gave a ring to a poor man who came to his door. When his wife reproached him for giving away such a precious ring with so large a stone, he had the poor man called back and warned him not to sell the ring for too little money.

Hearing of a devout and learned man who lived in great poverty, Rabbi Bunam had himself invited to the man's house as his Sabbath guest, had furnishings, dishes, and food taken to the empty house, and persuaded the man to accept new clothing. When he left, he gave his host a considerable sum of money, but the host refused it, saying he had already received more than enough. Rabbi Bunam explained the rest of what he had given was really to himself, "in order to heal the wound of pity which your wretchedness dealt me; only now can I really fulfill the commandment of charity." Only now could he truly give to his fellowman. "Join yourself to the afflicted and you will cleave to God," said Rabbi Mikhal of Zlotchov.[22]

The Hasidic community was a genuine caring community. This caring did not stop at the border of the particular Hasidic community, or even at the border of all the people of Israel. "Save the Jews," one zaddik prayed to God, "and if you cannot do that, save the goyim, and soon." Rabbi Mikhal of Zlotchov commanded his sons to pray for their enemies that all might be well with them and assured them that, more than all prayers, this is, indeed, the service of God.

Rabbi Zev Wolf of Zlotchov made it a rule that anyone could at any time come into his house and seat himself at his table. Once a man came in, sat down, and pulled out a large radish. His neighbors reproached him for his taproom manners, but Rabbi Wolf, who had overheard, called out that he felt like eating a really good radish. The radish eater experienced a sudden flood of happiness that swept away his embarrassment and offered Rabbi Wolf a handful of radish pieces.

When a number of zaddikim met in Lvov to discuss the corrupt ways of the new generation, and proposed to Rabbi Wolf that the renegades be forbidden to appeal to the court of arbitration, he asked them, "Do you think I love you more than them?"[23]

A rich and distinguished man in Nikolsburg, who was hostile to Rabbi Shmelke, tried to make him drunk before the evening of the Day of Atonement, in order to bring him to ridicule. Seized by the shuddering of the Days of Awe, Rabbi Shmelke threw off every vestige of wine. But in his sermon he prayed, "Even though there are persons who are hostile to me and try to make me an object of ridicule, forgive them, Lord of the world, and let them not suffer because of me." He said this in a voice so full of power that all present burst into tears. The rich and distinguished man turned to God and all his malice dropped from him.[24]

Love for enemies includes cherishing the enemy as part of one's "support system." Although Rabbi Bunam and Rabbi Meir of Stabnitz quarrelled for many years, when news of the latter's death was brought to Bunam, he jumped up, struck his hands together, and cried, "That is meant for me, for he was my support." Rabbi Bunam himself died that same summer. This understanding of enmity also means rejection of the "false peace" in which people try to end conflict without real resolution. When Rabbi Yitzhak of Vorki informed Mendel of Kotzk that their Hasidim had ceased quarrelling, the Kotzker rebbe grew angry, his eyes flashed, and he cried out: "So the power of deception has gained in strength and Satan is about to blot out the truth from the world!" Then the Rabbi of Kotzk pointed out to his bewildered friend that controversies in the name of Heaven spring from the root of truth, but a peace without truth—a peace which imposes pseudo-harmony to disguise conflict—is a false peace. Rabbi Bunam taught that we can find peace nowhere else than in our own selves. "When a man has made peace within himself, he will be able to make peace in the whole world."[25]

9

Healing and Helping

Rabbi Shlomo said: "If you want to raise a man from mud and filth, do not think it is enough to keep standing on top and reaching down to him a helping hand. You must go all the way down yourself, down into mud and filth. Then take hold of him with strong hands and pull him and yourself out into the light."[1]

*T*his description, to which we have referred before, has always seemed to me to express in a nutshell the paradox of all healing and helping. If we ask why it is not enough to stand above and reach down a helping hand, the answer is clearly that a person who sees you standing above him will not believe you can understand his problem well enough to help him. Once an opponent of Rabbi Bunam compelled two of his Hasidim to insult Bunam by asking how it was possible that he could be a rabbi when he spent his youth selling lumber in Danzig. Bunam replied that had he known what was ahead of him he would have spent his youth as his opponent had. But, he added, "it is better that I did not know." To his disciples he explained that Rabbi Meier had been a man of God from his youth on and did not know how to sin: "How can he know what is wrong with the people who seek him out? I was in Danzig and in the theaters, and know what sinning is like—and ever since then I have known how to straighten out a young tree that is growing crooked."[2]

Once when we were discussing "Climbing Down" in a group, a psychologist objected that he was not going to go out to where other people were. They had to come to his office. Also present was a doctoral tutee of his and mine who had been in Alcoholics Anonymous for 17 years. I asked him whether what AA calls the "twelfth step" was not just such a climbing down. The twelfth step involves going out to try to rescue someone whose sobriety is threatened and who wants you, a more seasoned recovered or recovering alcoholic, to help him or her resist the temptation. Our tutee confirmed in the strongest terms that it did involve just that, and described some hair-raising situations he had had to enter.

The risk, of course, is that the more seasoned recovered alcoholic will also lose his or her sobriety in the process of trying to help the endangered comrade. This brings us to the other part of the paradox. How does one avoid sinking into the "mud and filth" with the person one is trying to help, or even pulling that person down with you? How does one get the resources to go down into the pit and yet "take hold of him with strong hands and pull him and yourself out into the light"? "Healing," Buber suggests in the Postscript to *I and Thou* "is only possible to the one who lives over against the other, and yet is detached." Only the zaddik whose soul is unified can descend into the whirlpool, Buber pointed out in an early Hasidic book. It is along similar lines that Rabbi Zusya expounded the Talmudic saying: "The bold-faced go to hell, the shame-faced to paradise.":

> "Whoever is bold in his holiness, may descend to hell in order to raise what is base. He may roam about in alleys and marketplaces and need not fear evil. But he who is shamefaced, who lacks boldness, must keep to the heights of paradise, to studying and praying. He must beware of coming in contact with evil."[3]

This is not a question of mutuality, but of common experience with an extra dimension that the person who is helped does not have. Rabbi Bunam went to the theater, but he did not himself become a great sinner. Later, when he became the wise rabbi to whom people came for healing and help, he brought with him his earlier insight into the secular world that he had known, as Rabbi Meir had not.

The Baal Shem once said to a zaddik who used to preach admonishing sermons: "What do you know about admonishing! You yourself have remained unacquainted with sin all the days of your life, and you have had nothing to do with the people around you—how should you know what sinning is!" Another story tells how Rabbi Mikhal imposed a heavy and long penance on a man who had desecrated the Sabbath against his will because his carriage broke down. As a consequence, the man's body began to break down and even his mind was affected. Hearing that the Baal Shem was traveling through the region, the man turned to him, only to be given an incredibly light penance plus a message to Rabbi Mikhal to come to Chvostov the coming Sabbath. On the way to Chvostov, Rabbi Mikhal's carriage broke down, and he was too late to make it on foot by the beginning of the Sabbath. When the Baal Shem saw him cross the threshold, he said to him: "Good Sabbath, my sinless friend! You had never tasted the sorrow of the sinner, your heart had never throbbed with his despair— and so it was easy for your hand to deal with penance."[4]

The Hasidic attitude toward the unity of body and soul expressed itself in the healing performed by the zaddik. The unity of body and soul depends, Buber suggests, on the unity of the soul:

> The relation of a soul to its organic life depends on the degree of its wholeness and unity. The more dissociated the soul, the more it is at the mercy of its sicknesses and attacks, the more concentrated it is, the more it is able to master them. It is not as if it conquers the body; rather through its unity it ever again saves and protects the unity of the body.

The healing of the body takes place, accordingly, at the point where a crystallization and unification take place in a dispersed soul; for here "there takes place rapidly and visibly . . . what otherwise only grows in vegetative darkness, the 'healing.' " Occasionally, such an elemental moment of healing can come to a person from himself; but more often it is through the zaddik, the whole soul that comes to the aid of the dispersed one.

It is significant that in this connection Buber uses (in a 1921 essay) the term "psychosynthesis," which he clearly intends as a contrast to Freudian psychoanalysis:

> Through nothing else can this process be effected so simply and directly as through the psychosynthetic appearance of a whole, united soul laying hold of the dispersed soul, agitating it on all sides, and demanding the event of crystallization. It does not "suggest"; it fashions in the fellow-soul by which it is called, a ground and center, and the more genuinely and fully, the more it is concerned that the appealing soul that calls it does not remain dependent on it: the helper establishes ground and center not in order that he might install his own image in the soul that is to be rebuilt, but in order that it might look through him, as through a glass, into being and now discover being in itself and let it be empowered as the core of living unity.[5]

A striking example of this type of healing is the story in which the Baal Shem read aloud a passage from the Scriptures with the assistance of Rabbi Nahum of Tchernobil, who was at that time sickly, and plagued with all manner of aches and pains. "When the Baal Shem began to read, Rabbi Nahum felt pain leave one of his limbs after another with each successive part of the passage of reproof, and when the reading was over, he was rid of all his complaints: sound and well."[6]

If the soul which is relatively whole can save and protect the unity of the body, whereas the dissociated soul is at the mercy of its sicknesses, as Buber suggested, then it also follows that the healer whose soul is relatively more whole than that of the one to be healed can help the latter if he or she can give the person helped something of the personal wholeness that he or she lacks, "laying hold of the dispersed soul, agitating it on all sides, and demanding the event of crystallization." We cannot demand of the contemporary healer and helper that he or she be a zaddik; but we can expect that the healer has achieved a greater degree of personal wholeness than the one healed, so that we can speak of the former as one who, relatively speaking, has attained being and the latter as one who is in the process of becoming.

Rabbi Pinhas of Koretz likened the zaddik's descent into the "mud and filth" to the Lurian kabbalistic teaching of the vessels that broke because they could not bear the abundance of light poured into them. Only through this breaking did the light penetrate the lower worlds so that they did not remain in darkness. "It is the same with the breaking of vessels in the soul of the zaddik."

What this means in practice is shown by Rabbi Zusya of Hanipol. Once Zusya came to an inn where he saw long years of sin on the forehead of the innkeeper. Alone in his room he was overcome by "the shudder of vicarious experience" so that in the midst of singing psalms, he cried aloud, "Zusya, you wicked man! There is no lie that failed to tempt you, and no crime you have not committed," after which he enumerated the sins of the innkeeper as if they were his own, sobbing the while. The innkeeper, who had followed him, was at first seized with dull dismay. "But then penitence and grace were lit within him, and he woke to God." Zusya's experience was vicarious, but it was at the same time real. He did not play-act or try to work some technique. He really relived the sins as his own, and only through this "shudder" was he able to help the innkeeper. Another time, confronted by a person who refused to do penance, Zusya "climbed down all the rungs" until he was with the man and could bind the root of his own soul to that of the other. But then the other had no choice but to do penance along with Zusya, and it was great and terrible penance. When the man had stopped screaming, however, Zusya lifted him up and said, "Thine iniquity is taken away and thy sin expiated."[7]

The story of Zusya and his wife suggests a help which really grows out of mutuality; for here the help is not based on vicarious experience, but on Zusya's own plumbing of the depths of his personal situation. Zusya's wife was a shrew who kept nagging him for a divorce. Zusya's heart was so weighed down by her words that he wept. He showed her the tears on his pillow one night, and quoted the saying in the Talmud that the very altar sheds tears for a man when he puts away his first wife. "Do you still want a letter of divorce?" Zusya asked his wife, after which she grew quiet. "And when she was really quiet, she grew happy. And when she was happy, she grew good."[8] It is striking that she only grew happy after she grew quiet, but it is still more striking for our understanding of the person that it was only after she grew happy that she grew good and not the other way around! In any case, Zusya did not set out to help her. He appealed to her from the depths of his soul, and that appeal finally reached her.

One zaddik did not want the Messiah to come because he did not want to give up as lost all the souls that he might help through "climbing down" to where they were: "I stake my whole self for everyone, even the most unfaithful, and probe down to the root of his apostasy where wickedness can be recognized as need and lust. And if I get that far, I can pull him out all right!" Seen from the side of the one being helped, as one of the disciples of Rabbi Shlomo of Karlin pointed out, this means that one should show the rabbi what is bad, and not try to conceal it and show only what is good, as did the Hasidim of his time whom he described as "peasants of clay and cossacks of straw!" "For it is written that the priest shall look on the plague."[9]

The tales that show the zaddik lifting up the one who is healed and helped imply the personal wholeness of the zaddik and his resources for pulling himself and the other with strong arms into the light. A disciple of the great Maggid of Mezritch reported that all the desires of the disciples were fulfilled the moment they were within the limits of the town, or at least as soon as they entered the house of the maggid. "But if there was one among us whose soul was still churned up with wanting—he was at peace when he looked into the face of the maggid."[10] A more active form of help, not unlike a shock therapy, was reported when the Maggid laughed at every line of a list of sins that he had asked an old man to write down for him when the latter requested that he impose on him a penance for his sins. A rav who witnessed this could not understand the maggid's laughter until years later, when he heard someone quote a saying of the Baal Shem:

> It is well-known that no one commits a sin unless the spirit of folly possesses him. But what does the sage do if a fool comes to him? He laughs at all this folly, and while he laughs, a breath of gentleness is wafted through the world. What was rigid, thaws, and what was a burden becomes light.[11]

Another example of "shock therapy" is the story of Rabbi Hayke, a devout and learned man who lived as a hermit and mortified his flesh. Rabbi Aaron, a disciple of the Great Maggid, heard of him and preached so forcibly in the town near him that the hermit was drawn to come to hear his sermon. But all that he said was: "If a man does not grow better, he grows worse." These words bit into the mind of the ascetic like a poison which rouses the very core of life against itself. When he begged Rabbi Aaron to help him out of the maze of error in which he had lost his way, Rabbi Aaron sent him to his own teacher, the Maggid of Mezritch, with a letter. The maggid opened the letter and read its contents aloud: The man who was delivering the letter did not have a particle of sound goodness in him.

> Rabbi Hayke burst into tears. "Now, now," said the maggid.
> "Does what the Lithuanian writes really matter so much to you?"
> "Is it true or isn't it?" asked the other.
> "Well," said the maggid, "if the Lithuanian says so, it is, very probably, true."
> "Then heal me, Rabbi!" the ascetic begged him.
> For a whole year, the maggid worked over him and healed him.
> Later, Rabbi Hayke became one of the great men of his generation.[12]

A similar story is that of Rabbi David of Lelov who had done great penance for twice 6 years, fasting from one Sabbath to the next and subjecting himself to all manner of rigid discipline. When he went at the end of this time to visit Rabbi Elimelekh, the healer of souls, to discover what he must do to attain perfection, Rabbi Elimelekh twice ignored him, not even shaking hands with him when he shook hands with every one else. David of Lelov wept all night, and in the morning, despite himself, crept to the window and heard Rabbi Elimelekh preach of those who fast and torment themselves for a dozen years and then come to him to ask him to supply the little they still lack;

> But the truth of the matter is that all their discipline and all their pains are less than a drop in the sea, and what's more: all that service of theirs does not rise to God, but to the idol of their pride. Such people must turn to God by turning utterly from all they have been doing, and begin to serve from the bottom up and with a truthful heart.[13]

Rabbi David was so moved by these words that he almost lost

consciousness. Trembling and sobbing, he ventured onto the threshold, at which point Rabbi Elimelekh ran up to him, embracing and blessing him. When the zaddik's son protested that this was the very man whom he had twice ignored, Elimelekh answered, "No, indeed! That was an entirely different person! Don't you see that this is our dear Rabbi David!"

Even stranger is the story of young Jacob Yitzhak, later the Seer of Lublin who, when visiting a little town, heard the local *rav* recite the Morning Prayer with deep fervor, and later found that same fervor in all he did. When the *rav* told him he had never served a zaddik, Jacob Yitzhak was surprised; "for the *way* cannot be learned out of a book, or from hearsay, but can only be communicated from person to person." When he took the *rav* to see his own teacher, Rabbi Elimelekh, the latter turned to his window and paid no attention to his visitors. Jacob Yitzhak took the violently excited *rav* to the inn and returned alone.

"What struck you, my friend, to bring with you a man in whose face I can see the tainted image of God?" Elimelekh asked him, and explained that there is a place, lit by the planet Venus, where good and evil are blended. When ulterior motives and pride enter into a person's service of God, he comes to live in that dim place and does not even know it. He is even able to exert great fervor by fetching his blaze from the place of the impure fire and kindling his service with it. When the stranger was told these words, he recognized the truth in them, turned to God, ran weeping to the master, and was given help that enabled him to find the way.[14]

What is striking about this story is that at first glance it would appear that the stranger was doing the very thing that Hasidism most exalts: serving God with the "evil urge." Yet the motive, the *kavana* of the service is tainted, and the result is a "sublimation" which contains too much of the sphere of the planet Venus (one thinks of Wagner's *Tannhauser*!) or, in our terms, sex. The result is "patchwork," at best:

> From every deed an angel is born, a good angel or a bad one. But from halfhearted and confused deeds which are without meaning or without power angels are born with twisted limbs or without a head or hands or feet.[15]

In interesting contrast to this story stands the one of Rabbi Shlomo of Karlin who, while reciting psalms, was visited by "a man whose soul had become enmeshed in a tangle of oppressive impulses." When Rabbi Shlomo came to the words: "And hath delivered us from our oppressors," he turned to his guest, patted him on the shoulder, and asked: "Do you believe that God can wrest us from all oppression?" "I believe," said the man; and from then on, all disturbing impulses left him.[16]

At first glance, this seems to be a story of faith healing or, more precisely, of being healed through one's own faith, as when Jesus said to the woman who touched his garment and was healed of an issue of blood, "Thy faith hath made thee whole." To me, the heart of the tale lies elsewhere. What imprisons us all too often in the tangle of evil urges that oppress us is our guilt—our feeling of responsibility for having such impulses and an accompanying feeling of helplessness which becomes stronger in proportion to our guilt. Rabbi Shlomo of Karlin has suggested that instead we should look on them as something that oppresses us just as external tyranny and misfortune do. It is such a radical change in the way of looking at his disturbing impulses that enables the man to ascend to the faith that these oppressions too might be wrested from him by God. The faith is there, to be sure, but only after a genuine *metanoia,* a total change in the way of seeing one's existence.

A very different story of a cure is that of the beloved son of the Maggid of Koznitz who fell ill and whose father prayed for him, but not for his recovery, until Rabbi Levi Yitzhak of Berditchev heard of it and immersed himself in the bath with the holy intent of changing the maggid's trend of thought. Now with great fervor the maggid implored God to let his child recover. "At that time—so the hasidim say—not only little Moshe, the maggid's son, but all the sick children, far and wide, recovered."

Sometimes, as here, Hasidic healing is of a physical nature. At other times, as we have seen, it is spiritual, as in the testimony of a disciple of the Seer of Lublin that whenever a new Hasid came to him, the Seer "instantly took his soul out of him, cleansed it of all stain and rust, and put it back into him, restored to the state it had been in the hour he was born." Sometimes it is physical and spiritual together, as when Rabbi Moshe Leib performed a dance of healing for his friend the Rabbi of Berditchev when he learned that the latter had fallen ill. After his prayer for the zaddik's recovery, he put on his new shoes made of morocco leather and danced with such powerful mystery that "an unfamiliar light suffused the house, and everyone watching saw the heavenly hosts join in his dance."[17]

On the other hand, prayer, immersion baths, and holy dances are not always enough. When a disciple of Menahem Mendel of Kosov who was both well-to-do and fond of doing good deeds fell upon hard times, Rabbi Mendel sent him three times to his brother-in-law, Rabbi Uri of Strelisk, the "Seraph." Rabbi Uri offered to dedicate to him the merits of the immersion bath, his phylacteries, and his prayer. Rabbi Mendel sent him back with the message, "All this will not settle a single debt." The Seraph at once journeyed to Kosov and asked his brother-in-law what he wanted of him. "What I want," said Rabbi Mendel, "is for both of us to travel around for a number of weeks, and collect money from our people. For it is written: 'Thou shalt uphold him.' " And that is what they did.[18]

A final form of lifting the other up comes from that intuition that Martin Buber describes as "inclusion"—imagining the real, or experiencing the other side of the relationship. In contrast to both empathy and identification, inclusion means a bold imaginative swinging "with the intensest stirring of one's being" into the life of the other so that one can to some extent concretely imagine what the other person is thinking, willing, and feeling and so that one adds something of one's own will to what is thus apprehended. This means seeing through the eyes of the other and experiencing the other's side of the relationship *without* ceasing to experience the relationship from one's own side. Rabbi Mordecai of Neskhizh said to his son, "He who does not feel the pains of a woman giving birth within a circuit of 50 miles, who does not suffer with her, and pray that her suffering may be assuaged, is not worthy to be called a zaddik." When Rabbi Bunam's wife informed him that a whole carriage-load of Hasidim had come to see him, he exclaimed, "What are you thinking of? You know that that's not my business." But an hour later, after they had all left, he confessed: "I can't hold out against it any longer. The moment they came in, I knew the needs and wishes of every one of them.''[19]

A humorous story about inclusion is told of Yehiel Mikhal of Zlotchov. Once when he visited a city for the first time and was called on by prominent members of the congregation, he fixed a long gaze on each person's forehead and then told him the flaws in his soul and what he could do to heal them. The news of this got around, and the next visitors pulled their hats down to their noses to prevent his seeing the quality of their souls through looking at their foreheads. "You are mistaken," Rabbi Mikhal said to them. "An eye which can see through the flesh can certainly see through the hat."[20] Quoting this story in my book, *The Healing Dialogue in Psychotherapy,* I commented:

> Some people think of such gifts of seeing as magic powers. I rather think of it as being in touch—as touching, contact, a "dialogue of touchstones." If we keep in view the concrete reality of the between that underlies such intuition, we shall not be tempted to think of ourselves as *possessing* unusual powers. Those who feel they possess intuition sometimes try to use it for the spiritual or psychological domination of others. If we take seriously the "partnership of existence," the between, we shall not imagine that it is *our* power. What we contribute to the event is that we allow the intuition to happen between us and the other, rather than preventing it from happening by blocking it from our awareness, as is usually the case. But we cannot take credit for it. If the other person does not want to reveal him or herself to us at all, then this inclusive intuition will not take place. We cannot force the other to reveal himself.[21]

Transcribing these words, I am aware that the story appears to contradict what I have said. Rabbi Mikhal's second group of visitors did not want him to read their souls; yet he seemed ready to do so without their consent. Total mutuality in the process of therapy is neither possible nor desirable. Yet the zaddik often seems to arrive at his task of healing from such an exalted place that we might fairly wonder whether he has in fact climbed down into the mud and filth with the person he is helping. There is no gainsaying the great reverence in which the Hasidim held the zaddik, nor the fact that that reverence undoubtedly contributed to the effectiveness of the healing and helping. But precisely the fact that something must come first from the Hasid shows that there is, after all, an element of mutuality even in what Martin Buber properly describes, not only for pastoral care, but for teaching and psychotherapy, as a "normative limitation of mutuality." In the story in question, the visitors came of their own volition to see Rabbi Mikhal, and this coming, we may surmise, placed a demand on him other than any they consciously had in mind.

The healer and helper cannot remain above in lofty isolation but must, like Rabbi Elimelekh, who was sometimes accused of aloofness, be ready to go to the threshold to embrace "beloved Rabbi David." At the same time, the healer brings what, relatively speaking, we can call a "whole soul" to the encounter with one whose soul (and body) is not whole. And the healer and helper practices "inclusion," imagines the real, as the person who is helped cannot be expected to do for the healer.

Yet, as Martin Buber emphasized, the healer does not want the person being helped to become dependent but to find his or her own unique way through turning to a genuine relationship to being. It is not surprising, therefore, that a whole group of tales of healing and helping have no actual healer, but only the example and advice of the zaddik as to how one can help oneself.

One of the most interesting of these is Rabbi Pinhas of Koretz's advice concerning anger:

> Rabbi Pinhas once said to a Hasid: "If a man wishes to guide the people in his house the right way, he must not grow angry at them. For anger does not only make one's soul impure; it transfers impurity to the souls of those with whom one is angry."
>
> Another time he said: "Since I have tamed my anger, I keep it in my pocket. When I need it, I take it out."[22]

At first glance these two sayings appear contradictory. One warns against anger; the other implies that anger is sometimes needed. The key here is the difference between untamed anger and tamed anger. Untamed anger which tears through one, especially suppressed anger, which comes out as rage, makes one less of a person, and it also makes those who are attacked less, whether they express their own anger in turn or repress it. When one has reached a great personal integration, anger may be a legitimate expression of one's person which enhances rather than diminishes it. I do not mean that self-righteous anger in which one indulges when one imagines one is wholly in the right and the other wholly in the wrong. I mean anger as a demand placed upon the other in relationship *for the sake of the relationship*. This is not an anger that destroys. On the contrary, it confirms the other and is, when it is true, an expression of love for the other.

An equally striking saying is this teaching of Rabbi Zusya:

> God said to Abraham: "Get thee out of thy country, and from thy kindred, and from thy father's house, unto the land that I will show thee." God says to man: "First, get you out of your country, that means the dimness you have inflicted on yourself. Then out of your birthplace, that means, out of the dimness your mother inflicted on you. After that, out of the house of your father, that means, out of the dimness your father inflicted on you. Only then will you be able to go to the land that I will show you."[23]

One thing that is striking about this teaching is the suggestion that we are afflicted by a dimness which it is our life-task to remove. What Zusya means by 'dimness' we can only conjecture. Perhaps the hand that the Baal Shem spoke of that shuts out the wonders and mysteries of life, perhaps whatever prevents us from recognizing that the ground on which we stand is, like Jacob's stone in the wilderness, a ground of hallowing; perhaps our lack of awareness, our obtuseness, our insensitivity, our callousness toward what Abraham Joshua Heschel calls "radical amazement" and "the awareness of the ineffable." Whatever else it is, dimness is something that stands between us and our own life path. We are reminded of Franz Kafka's aphorism: "He felt that by merely existing he was blocking his own way"! It is certainly an existential equivalent for that neurotic suffering to which, as Freud pointed out, we prefer to cling rather than exchange it for everyday misery.

But the other thing that is striking about this teaching suggests a contrast with psychoanalysis: one does not begin by getting rid of the dimness that one's mother and father imposed on one but of the dimness that one has imposed on oneself. Like existential psychotherapy, this teaching recognizes that it is the attitude that we bring to what our mother and father "did" to us that imprisons us quite as much or more than our parents' actions or omissions themselves.

What is true of sickness is also true of healing. Our own attitude is even more important in our being healed than the gifts and goodwill of the healer. Rabbi Shlomo of Karlin once said to a man, "I have no key to open you," at which the man cried out, "Then pry me open with a nail!"[24] From then on, Rabbi Shlomo always warmly praised him. At the same time, the zaddik remains important as teacher and as example. Yitzhak Eisik of Kalev did not give advice to others as to how to endure pain, but set them an example himself:

> From youth until old age Rabbi Yitzhak Eisik suffered from an ailment which was known to involve very great pain. His physician once asked him how he managed to endure such pain without complaining or groaning. He replied: "You would understand that readily enough if you thought of the pain as scrubbing and soaking the soul in a strong solution. Since this is so, one cannot do otherwise than accept such pain with love and not grumble. After a time, one gains the strength to endure the present pain. It is always only the question of a moment, for the pain which has passed is no longer, and who would be so foolish as to concern himself with future pain!"[25]

10

The Limits of Helping

In the Ph.D. Program in Religion and Psychology that I directed at Temple University, one of the issues that I regularly stressed as arising from the meeting of religion and psychology was that of the limits of responsibility of the healer and helper in the therapy relationship. By responsibility, I mean not only professional but personal responsibility; not only accountability, but one's ability and one's duty to respond as a person in a mutual—though not fully mutual—situation. This is a topic on which many Hasidic tales touch in one way or another.

As we have already seen, because the zaddik does not want his Hasidim to become permanently dependent on him, he calls upon them to help themselves. Thus the Baal Shem pointed out that we say "God of Abraham, God of Isaac, and God of Jacob" rather than "God of Abraham, Isaac, and Jacob." "Isaac and Jacob did not base their work on the searching and service of Abraham," the Baal Shem commented. "They themselves searched for the unity of the Maker and his service." One New Year's Eve, Menahem Mendel of Rymanov entered the House of Prayer and surveyed the many people who had come together from near and far. "A fine crowd!" he called out to them. "But

I want you to know that I cannot carry you all on my shoulders. Every one of you must work for himself." According to Moshe of Kobryn, even God lets the flame of fervor go out, once it is kindled, so that the person who has been awakened to holiness "may act for himself and of himself attain to the state of perfect awakening." On New Year's Day, before the blowing of the ram's horn, the Rabbi of Kobryn used to call out: "Little brothers, do not depend upon me! Every one had better take his own part." In contrast to those zaddikim who prayed that those in need of help might come to them and find help through their prayers, Rabbi Naftali of Roptchitz prayed that those in need of help might find it in their own homes and not have to go to Roptchitz and be deluded into thinking that the rabbi had helped them.[1]

A part of the realism of the zaddikim was their recognition of the limits in those they wished to help. The Baal Shem expounded the statement that the Truth goes over all the world to mean that Truth is driven out of one place after another, and must wander on and on. The Seer of Lublin said that he loved the wicked who *knew* they were wicked more than the righteous who knew they were righteous. "But concerning the wicked who consider themselves righteous, it is said: 'They do not turn even on the threshold of Hell.' For they think they are being sent to Hell to redeem the souls of others."[2] One wonders to how many do-gooders and members of the helping professions these words apply!

The Seer's great disciple and antagonist the Yehudi saw the limits of every person as holy despair; something that needed to be recognized before it was possible for them to receive help from God:

> This is what the Yehudi said concerning the verse in the psalm: "How long shall I take counsel in my soul, having sorrow in my heart by day?"
> "So long as I take counsel in my soul, there must needs be sorrow in my heart by day. It is only when I realize that no counsel can help me, and no longer take counsel and know of no help save that which comes from God—it is only then that help is accorded me."
> And then he added: "This is the mystic meaning of the ritual bath."[3]

An equally important realism was the zaddik's recognition of the limits of his own power to help. Rabbi Israel of Rizhyn said of Rabbi Barukh of Mezbizh, "When a wise man went to the Rabbi Reb Barukh, he could spoon up the fear of God with a ladle, but the fool who visited him became much more of a fool." "This," Buber comments, "does not hold for this one zaddik alone." When Rabbi Meir Margaliot was beginning to study the Bible as a child, a man dressed in a short sheepskin appeared in the doorway and looked directly at him. Fearing the Evil Eye, Meir's mother snatched him down from the table in the middle of what he was saying. "It was I," the Baal Shem informed Rabbi Meir Margaliot years later. "In such hours a glance can flood the soul with great light. But the fear of men builds walls to keep the light away."[4] The way in which the persons who might be helped limit the help they might receive is expressed by the Baal Shem in the allegorical tale of *The Deaf Man:*

> Once a fiddler played so sweetly that all who heard him began to dance, and whoever came near enough to hear joined in the dance. Then a deaf man, who knew nothing of music, happened along, and to him all he saw seemed the action of madmen—senseless and in bad taste.[5]

The Baal Shem had a disciple who secretly wrote down all the teachings he had heard from him. One day the Baal Shem saw a demon going through the house carrying a book. When questioned, he said, "That is the book of which you are the author." The Baal Shem assembled his disciples, discovered who was taking notes, and studied for a long time the book the young man brought to him. Finally, he said: "In all this, there is not a single word I said. You were not listening for the sake of Heaven, and so the power of evil used you for its sheath, and your ears heard what I did not say."[6] An even more poignant recognition of the limits of the power of the helper to help is the statement that the Baal Shem interpolated in the middle of a sermon after he was shaken by a fit of trembling, such as sometimes seized him while he was praying:

> O, Lord of the world, you know that I am not speaking to increase my own reputation . . ." Here he stopped again, and then the words

rushed from his lips. "Much have I learned, and much have I been able to do, and there is no one to whom I could reveal it."[7]

Rabbi Pinhas of Koretz remarked that the people who came to hear his words of teaching were full of fervor on the Sabbath; but as soon as the holiness of the Sabbath was over, they were a thousand miles away from it. "It is as when a madman recovers: he is unable to remember what happened in the days of his madness." The Seer of Lublin, in marked contrast, recognized that there was something that 10 Hasidim could accomplish that the zaddik himself could not. Once a group of Hasidim took up a man who had been moaning on the bench and drank merrily with him until morning, as a result of which they averted the fate that the Seer had accepted that he should die on the Sabbath. Once the Seer confidently expected the Messiah to come that very year. When he did not, he commented that the rank and file of people either have turned completely to God or can do so. The real obstacle "is the superior people who . . . cannot attain humility, and therefore . . . cannot achieve the turning."

A very different note is sounded in the story, earlier noted, of the man who came to the Seer for help against alien thoughts which intruded while he prayed. The Seer told him what to do, but the man kept pestering him. Finally the Seer said: "I don't know why you keep complaining to me of alien thoughts. To him who has holy thoughts, an impure thought comes at times, and such a thought is called 'alien.' But you—you have just your own usual thoughts. To whom do you want to ascribe them?"[8]

In the above tales the zaddik's power to help is limited by his Hasidim. In some cases, however, it is limited by his own lacks or shortcomings. Martin Buber suggests that the turning point in the life of Abraham Yehoshua Heschel, the Rabbi of Apt, occurred when a respected woman came to ask his advice. The instant the Apter rebbe set eyes on her he shouted: "Adulteress! You sinned only a short while ago, and yet now you have the insolence to step into this pure house!" Then from the depths of her heart the woman replied:

> The Lord of the world has patience with the wicked. He is in no hurry to make them pay their debts and he does not disclose

their secret to any creature, lest they be ashamed to turn to him. Nor does he hide his face from them. But the Rabbi of Apt sits there in his chair and cannot resist revealing at once what the Creator has covered.[9]

From that time on the Rabbi of Apt used to say, "No one ever got the better of me except once—and then it was a woman."

In his Introduction to *The Later Masters,* Buber describes this turning point as learning that human justice fails when it attempts to exceed the province of a just social order and encroaches on that of direct human relationships: "Man should be just within the bounds of his social order, but when he ventures beyond it on the high seas of human relationships, he is sure to be shipwrecked and then all he can do is to save himself by clinging to love."[10]

Rabbi Moshe of Kobryn showed considerably more humility at the outset than the Apter rebbe. Once he laid his head on all the notes of request spread out before him, and said:

Lord of the world, "Thou knowest my folly, and my trespasses are not hid from Thee." But what shall I do about all these people? They think I really am something! And so I beg of you: "Let not them that wait for Thee be ashamed through me."[11]

There is a story that the Baal Shem spoke to a number of persons and each was sure that he alone was addressed. In a later generation, Rabbi Simha Bunam of Pshysha was very aware that he did not have this gift. "When my room is full of people, it is difficult for me to 'say Torah,' " he once remarked. "For each person requires his own Torah, and each wishes to find his own perfection. And so what I give to all I withhold from each."[12]

Still more somber notes are sounded by the zaddikim, notes that suggest that they too experienced what we describe as "burnout," when in their very desire to help they depleted their own resources. One such story is of the Seer of Lublin who once remarked: "How strange! People come to me weighed down with melancholy, and when they leave, their spirit is lighter." "But I myself," he added, and started to say, "—am melancholy," but paused and continued instead: "—am dark and do not shine." An even more poignant story is that of Rabbi Yehudah Zevi, who was afflicted with a disease which caused ulcers to break out all over his body so painfully that the doctors said it was impossible for a person to bear such pain. When one of the rabbi's close friends asked him about this, he confided that in his youth he prayed with all the force of his soul that the suffering might be taken from sick persons who came to him. "Later the strength of my prayer flagged and all I could do was to take the suffering upon myself. And so now I bear it."[13]

The most enigmatic and troubling of such stories is that told about Menahem Mendel of Kotzk, the famous Kotzker rebbe who spent the last 20 years of his life in seclusion. He was sometimes visited by Rabbi Yitzhak of Vorki, one of the very few admitted to him during the period when he kept away from the world. Once, after a long absence, Yitzhak of Vorki entered Mendel's room with the greeting, "Peace be with you, Rabbi." "Why do you call me rabbi," the Kotzker Rebbe grumbled. "Don't you recognize me? I'm the sacred goat."

> An old Jew once lost his snuffbox made of horn, on his way to the House of Study. He wailed: "Just as if the dreadful exile weren't enough, this must happen to me! Oh me, oh my, I've lost my snuffbox made of horn!" And then he came upon the sacred goat. The sacred goat was pacing the earth, and the tips of his black horns touched the stars. When he heard the old Jew lamenting, he leaned down to him, and said: "Cut a piece from my horns, whatever you need to make a new snuffbox." The old Jew did this, made a new snuffbox, and filled it with tobacco. Then he went to the House of Study and offered everyone a pinch. They snuffed and snuffed, and everyone who snuffed it cried: "Oh, what wonderful tobacco! It must be because of the box. Oh, what a wonderful box! Wherever did you get it?" So the old man told them about the good sacred goat. And then one after the other they went out on the street and looked for the sacred goat. The sacred goat was pacing the earth and the tips of his black horns touched the stars. One after another they went up to him and begged permission to cut off a bit of his horns. Time after time the sacred goat leaned down to grant the request. Box after box was made and filled with tobacco. The fame of the boxes spread far and wide. At every step he took the sacred goat met someone who asked for a piece of his horns.

Now the sacred goat still paces the earth—but he has no horns.[14]

If the sacred goat no longer has horns, then the tips of his horns no longer touch the sky and the connection between heaven and earth is broken. This is what the Kotzker rebbe implies has happened to him. If we take the story out of the humorous form of the snuffbox, we can assume that what Menahem Mendel really meant was that his Hasidim came to him with all the petty cares and burdens of their daily lives and that in the course of helping them, he lost his own connection with God or, even more important for him, was not able to work toward the reunification of God with his exiled Shekinah, the indwelling Glory or Presence of God which, according to the kabbalah, needs to be reunited with the *En Sof*, the infinite Godhead, for redemption to come. If we follow this line of thinking, we shall conclude not only that Menahem Mendel of Kotzk was "burned out" by his years of service, but also that he did not see the possibility of redeeming the world—reuniting God and his exiled Shekinah—through helping his followers raise the sparks fallen after the breaking of the vessels of light and surrounded by shells of darkness. If this is so, then "hallowing the everyday" could not, for the Kotzker— Martin Buber to the contrary—lead to that restoration of the sparks (*tikkun*) that presages redemption. We may legitimately wonder whether he made himself too available to his community and not enough to his own needs; whether his image of himself as zaddik and person led him to overextend himself; or whether his congregants disappointed him by not caring enough for the redemption of the Shekinah from its exile.

The Kotzker's withdrawal raises a profound question about the relationship between zaddik and Hasid and the help that the former can give to the latter. In some mysterious way, the healing process can be transformed into its opposite, and the one who is trying to heal may be lamed in that very process. I have always been enormously struck by the pathos of this story of *The Sacred Goat*, but never more so than when a dear friend, who had been for 20 years administrator and counselor in a small college, returned from a year's sabbatical and suffered a stroke that same day. Reflecting on how, through his tireless attention to detail and his personal counseling, he had been the very heart of that college during all those years, I found myself wondering whether his stroke had come to him on the very day of his return because his body and spirit rebelled against resuming this heavy burden. Not long after, I went up to him and told him the story. "You," I said, "are the Sacred Goat."

PART IV

"To Be Humanly Holy"

11

Dialogue and Trust

Although Hasidism grows out of a theosophy—knowledge about God—and a very detailed one, the Hasidim tended to lay greater stress on simple devotion to God. In order to persevere in the Hasidic way of life, one does not need a special grace, or faith in a set creed. But one does need trust—existential trust, trust in God, trust that God addresses us in the happenings of everyday life, and that we can make our lives real by responding to that address. For the Hasidim, as for biblical man, God's hiding was as real as his revealing himself, and when God hid himself it was difficult to maintain one's trust. The favorite disciple of Rabbi Pinhas complained to him that it was very difficult in adversity to retain perfect faith in the belief that God provides for every human being. "It actually seems as if God were hiding his face from such an unhappy being," he exclaimed. "It ceases to be a hiding," replied Rabbi Pinhas, "if you know it is hiding."

Shneur Zalman, the rav of Northern White Russia and the founder of the Habad, or Lubavitcher, Hasidism to which my mother's family belonged, once asked a disciple, "Moshe, what do we mean when we say 'God'?" The disciple was silent. After the rav had asked him a second and third time without response, he demanded the reason for his silence. "Because I do not know," replied the youth. "Do you think I know?" said the rav. "But I must say it, for it is so, and therefore I must say it: He is definitely there, and except for Him nothing is definitely there—and this is He." The rav could not define God, or describe his attributes, or even assert his existence in the abstract. But he could and did point in his dialogue with his disciple to meeting God in our actual existence in all its particularity.

A similar dialogue took place between Rabbi Bunam and his disciple Rabbi Hanokh. For a year, the latter had wanted to talk with Bunam every time he went into his house, but did not feel that he was man enough. Once, however, when he was walking across a field, and weeping, he knew that he must run to his rabbi without delay. Bunam asked him, "Why are you weeping?" "I am after all alive in this world," he confessed, "a being created with all the senses and all the limbs, but I do not know what it is I was created for and what I am good for in this world." His master did not reply by showing him the meaning of his life, or confirming his value in the world, but by revealing that this torment was one that he too could neither resolve nor dismiss: "Little fool," said Bunam, "That's the same question I have carried around with me all my life. You will come and eat the evening meal with me."

Hasidism takes over from the Lurian kabbala the doctrine of *tzimtzum*—the metaphor of God's self-limitation in the act of creation. The highest reality of the Divine, as Hasidism reinterprets *tzimtzum,* is not Meister Eckhart's impersonal Godhead, but the Absolute, who makes himself into a Person in order to bring man into relationship with him. "On account of his great love," says the Maggid of Mezritch, God limits his illuminating power in order that, like a father with his son, he may bring man stage by stage to where he may receive the revelation of the limitless original God."[22] God's relation to man and to creation is a voluntary contraction which in no way limits his absoluteness.

Father John M. Oesterreicher, the editor of the series of Catholic "Judeo-Christian Studies," *The Bridge,* sees the Hasidic doctrine of *tzimtzum* as an inferior conception which derogates from God's glory—a depreciation based upon a substantive and static misreading of the concept. Seen in its true dynamic and

interactive character, *tzimtzum* stands as one of the greatest re-
formulations of the biblical understanding of creation. It shows
God as at once separate from the world and man and yet in relationship to them, and in such a way that neither the separateness
nor the togetherness can be shown as either temporally or logically
prior. Creation, in this view, is the radical fact which establishes
and reestablishes the world, and behind which we cannot look to
any primal state before creation, or godhead before God. In our
own existence we can neither begin with our separate existence
as persons and then deduce our relations to others, nor begin with
our relations with others and then deduce our uniqueness as separate persons. Rather, we must begin with both at once. In our
relation to God, similarly, we cannot go back behind creation to
some more basic fact.

Yet this is just what not only the mystics, but also the theologians and the metaphysicians constantly attempt to do. Through
a logical analysis of the relationship between man and God, they
separate out the two factors of separateness and relatedness, and
then make one or the other of them prior. Paul Tillich rightly at-
tacks the theists for making God a person beside other persons.
But what he offers instead is no more satisfactory—a "Ground
of Being" that satisfies our logic's desire for a reality undergirding
man's relation with God and that at the same time forgives and
accepts as only a personal God could do! Alfred North Whitehead
and Charles Hartshorne, on the other hand, say that since God
cannot logically be both absolute and in relation, they prefer to
sacrifice the Absolute in favor of an imperfectly actual God who
attains his completion only through dialectical interaction with
the world. The Hasidic understanding of the relation of God and
the world does not have to fall into these logical either-or's. It
can bear paradox, because it sticks to the concrete given of our
existence, in which the seemingly irreconcilable opposites produced by our analytical thought exist together as a whole.

Revelation, to the Hasidim, did not mean the incursion of
the supernatural, but openness to the wonder of the everyday—
"the enormous lights and miracles" with which the world is filled.
Once a naturalist came from a great distance to see the Baal Shem
and said: "My investigations show that in the course of nature
the Red Sea had to divide at the very hour the children of Israel

passed through it. Now what about that famous miracle!" "Don't you know that God created nature?" answered the Baal Shem. "And he created it so, that at the hour the children of Israel passed through the Red Sea, it had to divide. That is the great and famous miracle!" "Miracle" is simply the wonder of the unique that points us back to the wonder of the everyday. If you fell through the ice and were saved at the last second from drowning, your knowledge of all the laws of heat and friction that might account for the ice melting at just that rate would not diminish by one jot the sense of wonder you would feel.

The Rabbi of Kobryn taught:

> God says to man, as he said to Moses: "Put off thy shoes from thy feet"—put off the habitual which encloses your foot, and you will know that the place on which you are now standing is holy ground. For there is no rung of human life on which we cannot find the holiness of God everywhere and at all times.[1]

The true opposite of "the habitual" is not the extraordinary, or the unusual, but the fresh, the open, the ever-new of the person who hallows the everyday. When Rabbi Bunam was asked why the first of the Ten Commandments speaks of God bringing us out of the land of Egypt, rather than of God creating heaven and earth, he expounded: " 'Heaven and earth!' Then man might have said: 'Heaven—that is too much for me.' So God said to man: 'I am the one who fished you out of the mud. Now you come here and listen to me!' "

It is only as persons that we can enter with our whole being into the dialogue with God that takes place in the heart of the everyday. To enter this dialogue means to hear and respond to God's "Torah," his guidance and direction in each hour of our lives. But it does not mean to freeze the Torah into a fixed, objective, universal law that demands only our external obedience, and not our unique response to a unique situation. The Rabbi of Kotzk heard his disciples discussing why it is written: "Take heed unto yourselves, lest ye forget the covenant of the Lord your God, which He made with you, and make you a graven image, even in the likeness of any thing which the Lord thy God hath bidden thee," and not, as they would have expected, "which the Lord thy God hath forbidden thee." The zaddik declared: "The Torah warns us not to make a graven image of anything the Lord our God has bidden us." Even divine Law and divinely sanctioned morality may become an idol which hides from us the face of God. By the same token, we cannot limit the address of the Torah to the Scriptures; for the word of the Creator speaks forth from the creation and the creatures each day anew. We can learn not only from what God has created but from what man has made, the Rabbi of Sadagora declared to his disciples.

> "What can we learn from a train?" one Hasid asked dubiously.
> "That because of one second one can miss everything."
> "And from the telegraph?"
> "That every word is counted and charged."
> "And the telephone?"
> "That what we say here is heard there."[2]

In the fifth chapter of his classic little book *The Way of Man According to the Teachings of the Hasidim,* Martin Buber retells Rabbi Bunam's story of Reb Eisik, son of Reb Yekel, who lived in Kracow, but who dreamt three times that there was a treasure buried beneath a bridge in Prague, and finally set out and walked the whole enormous distance to Prague. He found the bridge, but was afraid to approach it because of the soldiers who guarded it, until the captain of the guard noticed him and asked him kindly what it was he wanted. When he had told the captain his dream, the latter exclaimed, "And so to please the dream, you, poor fellow, wore out your shoes to come here!" If he had had faith in dreams, continued the captain, he would have had to go to Kracow when once a dream told him to go there and dig for treasure under the stove in the room of a Jew—Eisik, son of Yekel. When Rabbi Eisik heard this, he bowed, traveled home, dug up the treasure from under the stove, and built with it a house of prayer. The moral of this story, says Buber, is that the fulfillment of existence is only possible "here where one stands," in the environment which I feel to be natural, in the situation which has been assigned me as my fate, in the things that happen to me and claim me day after day. If we had power over the ends of the world and knew the secrets of the upper world, they would not give us that fulfillment of existence which a quiet, devoted relationship to nearby life can give us.

There is another aspect to this tale which Buber does not bring out, but which his life and my own and that of most moderns show to be essential. Perhaps if we had not gone to "Prague," we should not have discovered that the treasure was hidden beneath our own hearth. There is meaning in our searching, even when it takes us far afield, if it enables us to come back home to the unique task which awaits us. A young person raised in Judaism or Christianity is often barred from any genuine relationship to these religions by the fact that they are associated in his mind with the parents against whom he must rebel; with a social system the injustice of which is manifest; and often, in addition, with a shoddy way of presenting the religion that seems more concerned with group belonging or social snobbery than with anything genuinely religious. Such a person might find liberation in the teachings of Hinduism, Buddhism, or Zen Buddhism which he encounters unencumbered by relatives and institutions. After these have liberated him, he may be able to go back to find the treasure under his own hearth. When one does come back, it is with a new relationship such as only the fact of distancing makes possible.

This was my own experience in relation to Judaism. Brought up in a liberal Judaism of a very thin variety, I could never have returned to Judaism and established a new and deeper relationship with it had I not gone through Hinduism, Buddhism, Zen, Taoism, and Christian mysticism. Nor have I lost these other touchstones. They are part of the way in which I came to Hasidism and relate to it. Even if young people do not find their way back—and my own way to Hasidism was far more a way forward than a way back—they are still those who set out from Kracow. Whatever treasure they really find, however far it may be from home, is still bound to those original roots. These roots are embedded in the ground on which they stand and from which they respond to the new touchstones that call to them.

If man, to Hasidism, is a partner of the Creator, a co-creator who helps complete the creation by lifting the fallen sparks in the circle of existence allotted to him, he is by the same token a co-redeemer. The Rabbi of Kotzk surprised a number of learned visitors with the question, "Where is the dwelling of God?" "What a question!" they laughed. "Is not the whole world full of his glory!" But he answered: "God dwells wherever man lets him in." Rabbi Nachman of Bratzlav, the great-grandson of the Baal Shem, pictured human existence in terms of an angst as strong as any that Kierkegaard ever depicted:

> Let everyone cry out to God and lift his heart up to him as if he were hanging by a hair, and a tempest were raging to the very heart of heaven, and he were at a loss for what to do, and there were hardly time to cry out. It is a time when no counsel indeed can help a man and he has no refuge save to remain in his loneliness and lift his eyes and his heart up to God and cry out to him. And this should be done at all times, for in the world man is in great danger.[3]

But this very angst, this very loneliness becomes redemptive, as Buber suggests, by entitling the following saying of Rabbi Nachman "The Kingdom of God":

> Those who do not walk in loneliness will be bewildered when the Messiah comes and they are called; but we shall be like a man who has been asleep and whose spirit is tranquil and composed.[4]

The first saying is entitled "Prayer." Those who walk in loneliness do not wall themselves in in "demonic shut-in-ness," as Kierkegaard would say. They cry out to God. Even when they do not know how to pray, the silence beneath their words cries out:

> We know very well how we ought to pray; and still we cry for help in the need of the moment. The soul wishes us to cry out in spiritual need, but we are not able to express what the soul means. And so we pray that God may accept our call for help, but also that he, who knows that which is hidden, may hear the silent cry of the soul.[5]

In the end, redemption is neither the action of man alone, nor of God alone, but the completion of the dialogue between them. As Martin Buber said, in the last sentence of *I and Thou*,

"The event that from the side of the world is called turning is called from God's side redemption." If man's turning and God's redemption are two sides of one event, then the opposition that is so common between man's action and God's grace is a false one. This is not a matter of abstract theology, however, but of wholly concrete situations in which at times men have the resources to begin the turning and at other times not. Nowhere has this lability of the human situation vis-à-vis God been put more vividly than in a tale entitled "Turning and Redemption":

> The Rabbi of Rizhyn laid the fingers of his right hand on the table after the morning meal, and said: "God says to Israel: 'Return unto me . . . and I will return unto you.' " Then he turned his right hand palm up and said: "But we children of Israel reply: 'Turn Thou us unto Thee, O Lord, and we shall be turned; renew our days as of old.' For our exile is heavy on us and we have not the strength to return to you of ourselves." And then he turned his hand palm down again and said: "But the Holy One, blessed be he, says: 'First you must return unto me.' " Four times the Rabbi of Rizhyn turned his hand, palm up and palm down. But in the end he said: "The children of Israel are right, though, because it is true that the waves of anguish close over them, and they cannot govern their hearts and turn to God."[6]

This is not a statement about man's "sinful nature" and his dependence upon divine grace. It is a dialogue between man and God taking place in a concrete historical situation, the situation of exile when the resources to be "humanly holy" by serving God with the "evil" urge were at their lowest ebb, and the silent need of the soul cried out to God from beneath the waves of anguish. The love between man and God, like the love between person and person, is not a matter of merit or unearned grace but of the "between": If one loves less, then the other should love more for the sake of the relationship itself. It is in this spirit that we must understand one of the most moving of the Hasidic tales— one that at first glance gives the mistaken appearance of being close to the Pauline dualism between grace and law. This tale is entitled "The Judgment of the Messiah":

> A young man who lived in the days of the Great Maggid had quitted his father-in-law's house to go to the maggid. They had

fetched him back and he had pledged on a handclasp that he would stay at home. Yet shortly thereafter he was gone. Now his father-in-law got the rav of the town to declare that this broken promise was cause for divorce. The young man was thus deprived of all means of subsistence. Soon he fell ill and died.

When the zaddik had finished his story, he added, "And now, my good men, when the Messiah comes, the young man will hail his father-in-law before his court of justice. The father-in-law will quote the rav of the town, and the rav will quote a passage from the commentary on the Shulhan Arukh [the "Table of the Laws" codified by Joseph Karo in the sixteenth century]. Then the Messiah will ask the young man why, after giving his hand on it that he would remain at home, he broke his promise just the same, and the young man will say, 'I just had to go to the rabbi!' In the end the Messiah will pronounce judgment. To the father-in-law he will say: 'You took the rav's word as your authority and so you are justified.' And to the rav he will say: 'You took the law as your authority and so you are justified.'

"And then he will add: 'But I have come for those who are not justified.' "[7]

12

God Is Prayer

*P*rayer—nothing could be more central to Hasidic life, nothing more peripheral to contemporary life. Hasidic prayer, as I understand it, is the extension and deepening of the hallowing of the everyday. Prayer too is our way of becoming humanly holy.

"God is of no importance unless He is of supreme importance," wrote Abraham Joshua Heschel. Praying, therefore is not the road to enriching the self in either a material or a spiritual sense; for God and the relationship to God is not a means to our ends. "Prayer may not save us," wrote Heschel, "but prayer makes us worth saving." Theology, the definition of God, is not so important for prayer as our basic attitudes. In his beautiful essay on *Prayer,* one of the first of his writings that I ever read when he gave it to me in mimeographed form long before its publication, Heschel defines prayer as "an invitation to God to intervene in our lives"—"a perpetual inner attitude . . . the orientation of human inwardness toward the holy."[1]

Martin Buber defines prayer as "that speech of man to God which, whatever else is asked, ultimately asks for the manifestation of the divine Presence, for this Presence's becoming dialogically perceivable." The single presupposition of genuine prayer, according to Buber, is "readiness of the whole person for this Presence, simple turned-towardness, unreserved spontaneity": "He who is not present perceives no Presence." The special problem of prayer for the contemporary is that self-consciousness or awareness that I am *praying,* that *I* am praying that takes away this spontaneity and injures this statement of trust. This is an integral part of what Buber calls the "eclipse of God"—man's side of God's hiding when the "I" with all the "It" around it swells itself up and obstructs the road to the "Thou."[2] The Hasidic masters knew about this same problem of self-consciousness during prayer. "Disturbance from Within" is the title Buber gives to one such Hasidic saying about prayer:

> To commune with your Maker in solitude and silence, to recite psalms and pray to him—this it is good to do with your whole heart, until you are overwhelmed with weeping and weep to God as a child weeps to its father. But to weep according to plan in the midst of prayer—that is unworthy! He who does so can no longer say what he says with a whole heart, and the truly great weeping will not overwhelm him. Even thoughts about prayer are like "alien thoughts" which hinder the soul from fixing itself wholly upon God.[3]

One zaddik described the prayer which is most pleasing to God as an altar of silence. But he interpreted the biblical saying, "If thou make Me an altar of stone, thou shalt not build it of hewn stones, for if thou lift up thy tool upon it, thou hast profaned it," as a warning against lack of spontaneity in prayer: "If you do make an altar of words, do not hew and chisel them, for such artifice would profane it.[4]

My own definition of prayer is very simple and owes much to my two teachers and friends, Abraham Joshua Heschel and Martin Buber. Prayer, to me, is an attitude of openness to both the wonder and the claim of existence. "Alas, the world is full of enormous lights and mysteries," said the Baal Shem, "but man hides them from him with one small hand." Prayer is the removal of that hand. Prayer has to do with discovering each time and situation anew what we can bring and what can be brought—the way we bring ourselves to a life crisis, a poem, a dream, or a Hasidic, Zen, or Sufi tale. My chief adviser for my doctoral dissertation, Professor Arnold Bergstraesser, amazed me when I had finished it by asking, "Do you know Buber's secret? It is prayer." He did not mean by this that Buber spent so many hours a day praying, but that he brought himself every hour of his life in a real openness. This is what I think my former student and friend Silvio Fittipaldi means in his beautiful little book, *How to Pray Always Without Always Praying.*[5] This life of prayer can only be sustained if we bring ourselves to each situation with all we know and have been. We recall the Baal Shem's statement that the hose-maker who prayed the Psalms as he worked will be the cornerstone of the Temple until the Messiah comes.

In his essay on *Prayer,* Heschel tells the story of two towns, neither of which had a watchmaker. The first kept the clocks all going even though they knew the time was wrong. The second let all the clocks and watches stop. When a watchmaker finally came, he was able to repair and bring to the right time the clocks and watches of the first town but not of the second, where they had all rusted from disuse. The moral of Heschel's story was obviously that we should keep our prayer life going even if there was no "watchmaker" around to bring us in time with the Eternal, in the hope that one would eventually show up. But the situation of most of our contemporaries is that of the second town and not the first. What can be done about it? Many young Jews and non-Jews alike find prayer today in nontraditional forms where their parents could not—in the Hare Krishna society, in "Jews for Jesus," in Zen, yoga, or the Unification Church (the "Moonies"). But this is not really a continuation of or return to Heschel's first town—any more than I am an "atavism"—a throwback to my Hasidic great-grandfather in Lithuania—as my great-uncle Rabbi Charles Blumenthal thought when, at the age of eighty-one, he made a special trip from Waco, Texas, to Tulsa, Oklahoma, to meet the, to him, incomprehensible phenomenon of a young American Jew devoted to Hasidism.

Prayer is not simple. It is personal and communal, prescribed liturgy, and silent mediation. What Heschel says of Jewish prayer is perhaps true of all great prayer, namely that it is guided by the polar-opposite principles of "order and outburst, regularity and spontaneity, uniformity and individuality, law and freedom, a duty and a prerogative, empathy and self-expression, insight and sensitivity, creed and faith, the word and that which is beyond words." "A Jew never worships as an isolated individual," writes Heschel, "but as a part of the Community of Israel. Yet it is within the heart of every individual that prayer takes place."[6] Even when we pray alone—and we have our periods of quiet personal prayer, reciting the Psalms, turning silently and humbly to personal dialogue with God—we are also praying for the whole of Israel, for mankind, and for the redemption of the exiled Shekinah, or Presence of God, and the reuniting of God and the world.

Before praying, a person should prepare to die, taught the Baal Shem, because the intention of praying demands the staking of one's entire self. When the Baal Shem prayed, he often trembled. Once, what was usually just a slight quiver running through his body became a violent shaking and trembling; his face was burning like a torch, and his eyes were wide open and staring, like those of a dying man. Once, a disciple smoothed out his robe, and the disciple began to tremble too, and so did the table that the disciple held onto to steady himself. Another time, the water in the trough trembled, and still another time, the grain that filled open barrels nearby.[7]

Once Rabbi Pinhas of Koretz felt confused about his faith in God and traveled to the Baal Shem for help. The remedy, the Baal Shem told him, is to implore God to strengthen one's faith, as when Moses held his hands up during the battle against the Amalekites. Rabbi Pinhas's hearing of what the Baal Shem said was in itself a prayer, and in the very act of this prayer he felt his faith grow strong. A Hasid once traveling to Mezbizh to spend the Day of Atonement near the Baal Shem was interrupted on his journey, and had to pray alone in the open field when the stars rose. When he arrived in Mezbizh after Yom Kippur, the Baal Shem greeted him happily and said, "Your praying lifted up all the prayers which were lying stored in that field."[8]

Once, when the Baal Shem visited a town just before New Year's, and inquired about the manner of praying of the rav who read the prayers there in the Days of Awe, he was told that he recited all the confessions of sin in the most cheerful tones. When the Baal Shem questioned him, the rav explained: "The least among the servants of the king, he whose task it is to sweep the forecourt free of dirt, sings a merry song as he works, for he does what he is doing to gladden the king." "May my lot be with yours," said the Baal Shem.[9]

Rabbi Elimelikh of Lizhensk often looked at his watch when he recited the Prayer of Sanctification on the Sabbath in order to steady himself in time and the world when his soul threatened to dissolve in bliss. Rabbi Mordecai of Lekhovitz once complained that he had heard of a bird that sings its praise of God with such fervor that its body burst while he prayed and yet remained whole and sound. After a time the great fervor of his praying tore a hole in his lung. "I did not mean to say only one prayer in that way," he said to God; "I want to go on praying." Then God helped him and he recovered. Once, on the Eve of the New Year, when R. Moshe of Kobryn went up to the reader's desk to pray, he began to tremble in every limb and the pulpit to which he clung swayed back and forth. Finally he succeeded in driving his trembling inward and then stood firmly in his place and began to pray.[10]

But the zaddikim praised even more the prayer which was above fervor. Observing that his grandchild Israel made a habit of crying aloud while he prayed, Rabbi Barukh of Mezbizh asked him if he recalled the difference between a wick of cotton and a wick of flax. "One burns quietly and the other sputters!"[11] Once Rabbi Pinhas's disciples asked him why it was that when he prayed they could hear no sound and see no movement, so that he seemed to lack the fervor which shook the other zaddikim from head to foot. Rabbi Pinhas answered:

> Brothers, to pray means to cling to God, and to cling to God means to loose oneself from all substance, as if the soul left the body. Our sages say that there is a death which is as hard as drawing a rope through the ring on the mast, and there is a death as easy as drawing a hair out of milk, and this is called the death in the kiss. This is the one which was granted to my prayer.[12]

The son of Rabbi Shlomo Leib of Lentshno once asked his father how it was possible for a zaddik such as Rabbi Yitzhak of Vorki to pray quietly and simply without giving any sign of ecstasy. "A poor swimmer," answered Rabbi Shlomo Leib, "has to thrash around in order to stay up in the water. The perfect swimmer rests on the tide and it carries him."[13]

To many of the zaddikim, the true prayer was not for one's own needs, but for the redemption of the *Shekinah,* God's exiled presence, the reunion of God and his world. Once Rabbi Barukh's grandson was playing hide-and-seek with a friend and came crying to his grandfather because his friend ran away and did not try to find him. At this, Rabbi Barukh's eyes brimmed with tears, and he cried, "God says the same thing: 'I hide, but no one wants to seek me.' "

The prayer a person says is, in itself, God, taught Rabbi Pinhas: "He who knows that prayer in itself is God, is like the king's son who takes whatever he needs from the stores of his father." On the first day of the New Year festival, Rabbi Shmelke of Nikolsburg prayed, with tears in his eyes, complaining that the people prayed for nothing but their own needs when they prayed and did not think of the exile of God's glory. On the second day, he wept, and said that the Messiah did not come on the first or on the second day "because today, just as yesterday, all their prayers are for nothing but . . . the satisfaction of bodily needs!" Another time, he said that the Messiah Son of David will not come until "the tears of Esau"—the tears which all human beings weep when they pray for something for themselves—have ceased to flow, and the people weep instead because the Divine Presence is exiled, and because they yearn for its return.[14]

Rabbi Naftali of Roptchitz told of a soldier who saved the life of the Czar and who was told to ask for any favor he pleased. When he complained that his sergeant was brutal and asked that he be transferred to another, Czar Nicholas cried, "Fool, be a sergeant yourself!" "We are like that," said Rabbi Naftali: "we pray for the petty needs of the hour and do not know how to pray for our redemption."[15] To fully appreciate this last story, we must bear in mind that redemption, for Hasidism, as for Judaism in general, does not mean individual salvation but the redemption of the whole of God's creation, the reuniting of God with his exiled *Shekinah.*

From the Baal Shem onward, the chief characteristic of Hasidic prayer was bringing one's whole soul and life into prayer.

Prayer, to the zaddikim, as to Martin Buber, was a dialogue of the worshiper with God. Rabbi Israel of Koznitz testified to his son Moshe that alien thoughts came to him only when he was praying. "With the help of God I brought them all home to their source and their root, to where their tent stood in the beginning of time." When the Seer of Lublin was reproached for taking a pinch of snuff while praying, he told the story of a king who was so pleased by the song and harp-playing of a ragged street singer that he took him into his palace and listened to him day after day. Reproached by a courtier for stopping to tune his harp in the middle of praying, the harpist answered that the king had many people better than he in his orchestras and choirs. "But if they do not satisfy him and he has picked out me and my harp, it is apparently his wish to endure its peculiarities and mine." Rabbi Zevi Hirsh of Rymanov taught his disciples that they should sing to God when they rose in the morning and saw that God had returned their souls to them, and he told of a Hasid who, whenever he came to the words in the Morning Prayer, "My God, the soul you have placed in me is pure," danced and broke into a song of praise.[16] One zaddik went further and asserted that one sings unto God in order to bring about that God sings in us![17]

When a Hasid complained that he did not understand the statement "I believe with perfect faith" since "If I really do believe, then how can I possibly sin? But if I do not really believe, why am I telling lies?", Rabbi Noah explained that the words "I believe" are really a prayer, meaning "Oh, that I may believe!" Suffused by a glow from within, the Hasid cried, "That is right! Lord of the world, oh, that I may believe!" Rabbi Moshe of Kobryn, whenever he came to the words in the seder about the youngest son who does not know how to ask, always paused, sighed, and said to God: "And the one, alas! who does not know how to pray—open his heart so that he may be able to pray." Rabbi Yisakhal Baer of Radoshitz taught that man's prayer is God's prayer; for God not only takes pleasure in the prayer of righteous men, but wakens those prayers within them and gives them the strength to pray. The Kotzker rebbe advised a Hasid who told him about his poverty and troubles not to worry, but to pray to God with all his heart. When the Hasid replied that he did not know how to pray, pity surged up in the Kotzker and he said, "Then you have indeed a great deal to worry about."[18]

Once a Hasid complained to Rabbi Yitzhak Meir of Ger that he had prayed for 20 years, and his praying was no different from when he started. The Rabbi of Ger reminded him of the teaching that one should take the Torah on oneself as the ox takes the yoke. "You see, the ox leaves his stall in the morning, goes to the field, plows, and is led home, and this happens day after day, and nothing changes with regard to the ox, but the plowed field bears the harvest."[19] The purpose of prayer is not rising to higher spiritual planes, but having a dialogue with God.

At New Year's, said Rabbi Pinhas, everyone can see God according to his own nature: one in weeping, one in prayer, and one in the song of praise." Once Rabbi Zusya prayed, "Lord, I love you so much, but I do not fear you enough! Let me stand in awe of you like your angels, who are penetrated by your awe-inspiring name." God answered Zusya's prayer, and his name penetrated Zusya's heart. But Zusya crawled under the bed like a little dog and shook with animal fear, howling, "Lord, let me love you like Zusya again!" And this prayer too was granted.[20]

13

The World of Death

Because the zaddikim were so close to life, they also offer us profound insight into death—not through doctrines, but through their own life experiences, and this experience varies from zaddik to zaddik. On his way to his dying teacher, Rabbi Shlomo of Karlin, who had bid him come that he might consecrate him to leadership, Rabbi Mordecai of Lechovitz suddenly felt as if a rope across an abyss gave way and he was falling through shoreless space. "I have been severed from my teacher," he screamed, after which he did not utter another word but was quite out of his mind. When he was told that his teacher was dead, instead of harming himself, as some feared, he regained his composure, pronounced the benediction, and cried, "He was my teacher, and he shall remain my teacher."[1]

In the month he was to die, the Apter rebbe discussed at his table the death of the religious man. After walking back and forth in the room, his face glowing, he stopped by the table and said, "Table, pure table, you will testify in my behalf that I have properly eaten and taught at your board." Later he asked that his coffin be made out of the table. A very different story of the death of a zaddik is that of Rabbi Bunam and his son Abraham Moshe.

When Abraham Moshe heard his father recite the Evening, Morning, and Afternoon Prayer in succession, he fainted and hit the floor with the back of his head, after which he retired to his room and would not come out to see his sick father, even though his mother pleaded with him. When his mother pleaded with Rabbi Yitzhak of Vorki to intervene, he objected that the father and son were concerned with something in which no one could meddle. At the very moment that Rabbi Bunam died, his son opened his eyes and said, "Now there is darkness all over the world." Later Abraham Moshe said to his mother that he had a craving to die. When she protested that one had to learn how to die and learn it long and properly, he answered, "I have learned long enough" and lay down. After he died, his mother learned that he had visited his favorite disciples and taken leave of them.

Another story: A Hasid of Rabbi Menahem Mendel of Vorki reported the death of a zaddik as "very beautiful. It was as though he went from one room into the next." "No, from one corner of the room into another corner," rejoined Rabbi Mendel. When the Baal Shem died, he said, "I have no worries with regard to myself. For I know quite clearly: I am going out at one door and I shall go in at another." "Man is always passing through two doors," said Rabbi Bunam: "out of this world and into the next, and out and in again." "Death is merely moving from one home to another," said the Kotzker rebbe. "If we are wise, we will make the latter the more beautiful home."[2]

Once Rabbi Zusya said to the earth: "Earth, Earth, you are better than I, and yet I trample on you with my feet. But soon I shall lie under you and be subject to you." Rabbi Pinhas of Koretz said: "My teacher, the Besht, realizing the imminence of his death, exclaimed: 'Lord of the Universe, I make Thee a gift of the remaining hours of my life.' This is true martyrdom for the sake of the Lord." When a *rav* asked the Tzanzer rebbe why the Holy House of God was built on Mount Moriah, where Abraham was asked to sacrifice Isaac, rather than on Mount Sinai where the Torah was given, the rabbi replied: "The place where a man served his God in readiness to die for Him, is dearer to the Lord than even the place where the Torah was received." The holy Yehudi said: "A man should choose two mitzvoth that he may perform them with his whole heart and soul, and even be ready to die for them." But the Magelnitzer added, "Choose one mitzvah for which you are ready to die, namely the mitzvah which you are in the act of performing," thereby changing the Yehudi's emphasis from a timeless hierarchy to being totally in the present.[3]

Readiness to die does not mean that death or martyrdom is valued in Hasidism over life. A disciple of Rabbi Naftali of Roptchitz recited the Lamentations every midnight with such overwhelming sorrow that, when Naftali took the other disciples to see him lying on the bench in a deep sleep, at the stroke of midnight he tore open his shirt collar and cried out: "Mother, I am burning up!" When he left Naftali for the Apter rebbe, Naftali was much grieved: "With all my strength," he said, "I tried to keep down the fire. With the rabbi of Apt he will be a burnt offering in the conflagration of his heart." Soon after this, Rabbi Feyvish died in the House of Prayer while saying the prayer, "The breath of all that lives shall bless your name." If the death of the ecstatic was a cause of grieving to Rabbi Naftali, the death of an ascetic was sometimes a cause of scorn. When a rabbi was told that a certain man had died of hunger, he replied, "No, he died of pride."[4]

Shortly before his death, Shneur Zalman, the *rav* of Ladi, asked his grandson whether he could see anything. When the boy looked at him in astonishment, the *rav* said: "All I can still see is the divine nothingness which gives life to the world." One evening at the wailing wall in Jerusalem, a zaddik saw a tall woman veiled from head to foot who was weeping softly to herself. With tears in his own eyes, the zaddik exclaimed, "For whom can the *Shekinah,* the Divine Presence, be mourning, if not for Rabbi Pinhas of Koretz!" He tore his robe and said the blessing for the dead.[5]

There are other remarkable reports of the way in which the zaddikim respond to the death of others. After the death of his son, Levi Yitzhak of Berditchev danced on the way to his funeral. When his disciples expressed astonishment, Levi Yitzhak exclaimed, "A pure soul was given to me. A pure soul I render back." When Rabbi Menahem Mendel of Rymanov's daughter died soon after his wife, Rabbi Mendel said to God, "Now I have no one left to rejoice in, except you alone. So I shall rejoice in you." And he said the Additional Prayer in a transport of joy.[6]

Rabbi Leib, son of Sarah, the wandering zaddik, used to visit Pinhas of Koretz several times a year, despite the great difference in their manner of work, one traveling and doing his work in secret and the other working openly in one place. Once when the two men closeted themselves together after the Day of Atonement, Rabbi Pinhas emerged with his eyes streaming with tears, and his Hasidim heard him say, "What can I do since it is your will to go first?" That year, as I related earlier, Rabbi Leib died toward the end of the winter and Rabbi Pinhas the summer following.

On Simhat Torah, the Day of Rejoicing in the Law, the Rabbi of Ulanov, a dear friend of Naftali of Roptchitz lay dying. In the midst of the great round dance that Naftali's Hasidim were executing in the court of the zaddik's house, Naftali suddenly raised his hand and kept silent like someone overcome by bad news. But then he cried to his Hasidim that they should rejoice and dance just as the soldiers continue to fight when one of the generals dies in battle. Later it became known that the Rabbi of Ulanov had died that very hour.[7]

My friend, the distinguished American poet Denise Levertov, tells of how her father (whose early book on Hasidism in German I myself read years ago) danced at the hour of his death and how she learned later that that was the very time she herself had felt impelled to go out and dance in her garden.

Rabbi Moshe of Kobryn once expressed astonishment that at the time of Moses the people of Israel, in their greatest hour, "refused to hear the voice of God for fear of death that is nothing but a wresting of the soul from its husk to cling to the light of life!" He repeated the question twice, fainted away and lay motionless, but when he revived added: "It was very hard for them to give up serving God on earth."

When a man expressed the wish, in the presence of the Belzer rabbi, to die like a good Jew, the zaddik commented: "Such a wish is wrong. Desire rather that you may live like a good Jew, and it will follow as a consequence that you will die like a good Jew." Death too is a part of the hallowing of the everyday—not kiddush *haShem* (martyrdom) but kiddush *hahayim* making life holy! When Rabbi Bunam's disciples laughed at one of their number who had lost his scarf and looked all over for it, Rabbi Bunam said, "He is right to treasure a thing which has served him. Just so after death the soul visits the body that has sunk and leans above it." "Before dying," Bunam commented once, "all the powers of the body clutch hard at life." Bunam expounded the biblical account of the fall of Adam by picturing God in the fullness of his mercy as permitting human beings to live in "the world of death" so that they might achieve perfect redemption. "That is why he decided to prevent them from taking also of the tree of life, for then their spirit would never have fought free of matter and prepared for redemption."[8]

Rabbi Yitzhak Meir of Ger's explanations of why we weep at the words in the prayer, "Man, his origin is of the dust and his end is in the dust," is intriguing: "The origin of the world is dust, and man has been placed in it that he may raise the dust to spirit. But man always fails in the end and everything crumbles into dust." In some contrast to this tale is his deeply moving interpretation of the reason why the Talmudic sages said we must love God with all our heart and soul, "even if He takes our soul," but did not add "even if he takes our heart." "If God so desires, let him take our life, but he must leave us that with which we love him—he must leave us our heart." Buber entitles this tale "The Heart Remains".[9]

When I was in high school, I once said to my girlfriend that my whole goal in life was to live long enough to develop a philosophy that would enable me to accept death. Since I have come to know the tales of the Hasidim, I have often been struck by the resemblance between my statement and the Hasidic tale "The Meaning":

> When Rabbi Bunam lay dying his wife burst into tears.
> He said: "What are you crying for? My whole life was only that I might learn how to die."
> When the Baal Shem died, he said, "Now I know for what I was created."[10]

When we live with the death of one who was close to us, we know that the mystery of his having existed as a person, and being with us no longer, cannot be plumbed. It is part of the paradox of personal existence itself, which has no secure or continuous duration in time yet does really exist again and again in moments of present reality. We tend most of the time to think of death as an objective event that we can understand through our categories. But when we truly walk in the valley of the shadow, the imminence of death tells us something that we have really known all along: that life is the only reality that is given to us, that this reality—and not some continuing entity or identity of a personal nature—is all that we actually know. We do not know life without our individual selves, but neither do we know our selves without life. We know death, to be sure, but we know it as death-in-life. Life is the reality in which we share while we are alive. "In order really to live," said Rabbi Yitzhak, the zaddik of Vorki, "a man must give himself to death. But when he has done so, he discovers that he is not to die—but to live."[11]

14

Hope and Despondency

> Strength beyond hope and despair,
> Climbing the third stair.
> —T. S. Eliot

Hope and despondency are related to what in *Touchstones of Reality* I have called the "courage to address and the courage to respond."[1] Hope implies the presence of that courage, despondency its absence. The simplest and most familiar form of hope and despondency is the emotional complement of expectation and disappointment—what the Buddha called the "hankering and dejection common to the world." "What a good and bright world this is if we do not lose our hearts to it," cried a Hasidic master, "but what a dark world, if we do!" Expectation and disappointment point, in their turn, to understanding hope and despondency as the tension between the present and the future, or between the past and the future. This may be hope or despondency over improving oneself or one's lot, or hope of progress as opposed to the despondency that sees one as fixated in the present or, still worse, the past. But it may be, too, that we shall have to go through despondency in the present in order to reach hope in the future. "Wait without hope/For you are not ready for hope," as T. S. Eliot suggests in *Four Quartets*. The Hasidim speak of a "between-stage," in which we must first change into nothing if we want to change from one reality to another. To become a new creature, we must cease to be the creature that we are. In this sense despondency might be seen as the fruitful darkness between the light of past and future hope. When Rabbi Pinhas was asked why tradition holds that the Messiah will be born on the anniversary of the destruction of the Temple, he replied:

> The kernel which is sown in earth must fall to pieces so that the ear of grain may sprout from it. Strength cannot be resurrected until it has dwelt in deep secrecy. To doff a shape, to don a shape— this is done in the instant of pure nothingness. In the husk of forgetting, the power of memory grows. That is the power of redemption. On the day of destruction, power lies at the bottom of the depths, and grows. That is why, on this day, we sit on the ground. That is why, on this day, we visit graves. That is why, on this day, the Messiah is born.[2]

But it may be that real hope is not tied to the future at all, that it resides, on the contrary, in the present. Only living in the present is the antidote to that unsound expectation that ties us forever to the future and makes it inevitable, as Pascal said, that we should be forever unhappy.

> Soon after the death of Rabbi Moshe, Rabbi Mendel of Kotzk asked one of his disciples:
> "What was most important to your teacher?"
> The disciple thought and then replied:
> "Whatever he happened to be doing at the moment."[3]

These reflections take us into one of the most difficult and important considerations, namely, how to distinguish between true and false despondency. Some would say, between true sorrow and false despondency, since there are those who would not recognize *any* despondency as true. False sorrow and false joy ignore one's real lack and are, therefore, static. True sorrow and true joy know one's real lack and are, therefore, "ongoing."

The Rabbi of Berditchev said:

"There are two kinds of sorrow and two kinds of joy. When man broods over the misfortunes that have come upon him, when he cowers in a corner and despairs of help—that is a bad kind of sorrow, concerning which it is said: 'The Divine Presence does not dwell in a place of dejection.' The other kind is the honest grief of a man who knows what he lacks. The same is true of joy. He who is devoid of inner substance and, in the midst of his empty pleasures does not feel it, nor tries to fill his lack, is a fool. But he who is truly joyful is like a man whose house has burned down, who feels his need deep in his soul and begins to build anew. Over every stone that is laid, his heart rejoices."[4]

"The worst thing that the Evil Urge can achieve," said Rabbi Shlomo, "is to make a man forget that he is the son of a king." This false despondency is related to our failure to accept the creative possibility of the new moment. Our greatest crime is not that we sin, said Rabbi Bunam, but that we *can turn* every moment, and do not.

The Seer of Lublin loved gaiety and hated dejection, and for this reason he rejoiced over the merry sinner who, instead of repenting and being sorry before returning to his folly, as most people do, knows neither regrets nor doldrums and radiates happiness from the tower of his being. To forget gladness and fall into a depression is to forget God, said another Hasidic rebbe. "A broken heart prepares man for the service of God, but dejection corrodes service." What is called for, clearly, is to walk a narrow ridge between true and false despondency. Rabbi Moshe Leib of Sasov was spoken of by Rabbi Bunam as a man whose heart was broken and crushed yet sound and whole.[5] Our personal wholeness is not the original innocence and intactness of the child who has not yet ventured into life, but that healing and restoration that is attained through giving oneself fully to life with all its heartbreak. As my friend Virginia Shabatay has said, "In the very act of living/loving—exposing oneself—one gains one's true wholeness."

There is a certain self-indulgence in despondency, a failure to take fully seriously one's situation in the world. "I often hear men say: 'I want to throw up the world,' " said the Rabbi of Ger, whom I have earlier quoted. "But I ask you: Is the world yours to throw up?" To know what one lacks is to know what one needs to move on. But there is a false heart-searching which fixes one where one is and says, "I shall never get out of the situation or fault in which I find myself." The sages of the Talmud said: "Reflect upon three things: know whence you have come, where you are going, and to whom you will sometime have to give account and reckoning." But when Esau asks what seem to be the same questions, it brings heaviness into the human heart.[6]

All this implies that there *is* such a thing as true despondency. The Seer of Lublin observed that people came to see him weighed down with melancholy and that when they left him they were lighter, "although I myself . . . am dark and do not shine." The zaddik is often pictured, indeed, as one upon whom sorrow descends in order that he may not lose touch with the people, yet he is, at the same time, one who finds God even in sorrow. After the Rabbi of Rizhyn reached the summit, he had to descend time and again into the condition of dejection "in order to redeem the souls which had sunk down to it."[7] Sometimes even the zaddik cannot hope but can only plead with God.

A "narrow ridge" is what we must also walk if we are to distinguish between true and false hope. One form of false hope is that stoicism that leads us to settle down in an intolerable situation rather than try to change it. "The real exile of Israel in Egypt is that they had learned to endure it," said Rabbi Hanokh. The Hasidim go even further and claim that a hope without zeal or ecstasy is not a true hope. He who has not felt the blaze of ecstasy in this world does not feel it in paradise. When Rabbi Schneur Zalman's teacher, Rabbi Abraham the Angel, walked with him through the city gate, he called to the coachman, "Urge on your horses and let them run until they forget they are horses." Schneur Zalman took these words to heart and realized that he had not yet learned to serve God with "ardent zeal." He turned back to the city and remained with Rabbi Abraham for another year.[8]

There is, according to the Yehudi, as we have seen, a "holy despair" in which one ceases to take counsel with oneself and knows of no help save that which comes from God. This does not mean that one does nothing, but that what one does, one does wholeheartedly, without calculating the profit and the loss. One

Hasidic tale distinguishes between true turning, which is done *without* hope but with the heart, and false turning, which is done with the hope of calculation but without the whole heart:

> This is the nature of turning: When a man knows he has nothing to hope for and feels like a shard of clay because he has upset the order of life, and how can that which was upset be righted again? Nevertheless, though he has no hope, he prepares to serve God from that time on and does so. That is true turning and nothing can resist it. That is how it was with the sin of worshiping the golden calf. It was the first sin and the people knew nothing of the power of turning, and so they turned with all their heart. But it was different with the sin of the spies. The people already knew what turning can accomplish, and they thought that if they did penance they would return to their former state; so they did not turn with all their hearts, and their turning accomplished nothing.[9]

True hope is not to resign oneself to the will of God but to take courage and strength. One need not see the medicine life dispenses as sweet. If it is bitter, it should be recognized as such. Yet to say it is bitter is not to say it is bad. "A man should be like a vessel that willingly receives what its owner pours into it, whether it be wine or vinegar." There are some pious persons who waste their life energies trying to pretend to themselves that vinegar is really wine. That we are not asked to do. When we grow old, we recognize that melodies that once made our heart leap have lost their savor. And we recognize that we too lose our savor. But even this may be a good thing: "When I see that after all I have done I am nothing at all, I must start my work over again." Or as Martin Buber said, "It is a glorious thing to be old if one knows how to begin anew. Not to be young, but to be old in a young way."[10]

An important test for distinguishing true and false hope and true and false despondency is whether it is in relation to oneself or to all. Only when we weep because the Divine Presence is exiled and we long for its return, will the Messiah come. For *whom* do we hope and for *what* do we hope? For ourselves or for the task we are called to perform? If we think in terms of ourselves alone, we are bound to fall into despondency. Our lives seem an endless round of toil and trouble, ending in death. If we find meaning in our task, then we may hope even when our efforts are crowned with no other success than their ineradicable existence as real events within the passage of time.

A few years ago I met with a group in Santa Barbara for an afternoon's discussion. A psychoanalyst in the group suggested that I should speak about my work on *Martin Buber's Life and Work*—books that had been "in progress" for over 12 years with a first volume completed 9 years before. I spoke of the difficulties caused by conventional conceptions of a "biography" and of the difference between a monological, process approach to a person's life and a dialogical, event-centered approach. But the group proved more interested in why I was having trouble completing this task. One person, himself a professor and writer, picked up on my statement that my book *Martin Buber: The Life of Dialogue* had won wide attention and universal acclaim when it was published over 20 years before. He suggested that my difficulties might be related to the fact that I could expect no such response to my forthcoming Buber book. Yet I did not write the earlier book in order to get a response but because I wholeheartedly believed in it. It was rather the tension between hope and despondency which stood in the way of my bringing to this new task the fervor and wholeheartedness of my youth, and this was not just the hope for any particular book. What weighed on me, then, was the enormous effort I had expended over the past quarter of a century—the thousand one-night stands at lectures, the giving to worthwhile persons and causes which did not replenish my depleted life energy, that store of spontaneity which is the *promise* of present and future. Perhaps it was my whole life that weighed in the balance.

To write my book, I had to overcome *both* expectation and despondency. The former can be overcome through realism— through the realization that the future is of value only if it grows organically out of a present that has value and reality in itself. But how can we overcome despondency—the refusal of the forces within us to plunge together into an ecstasy that will take us beyond ourselves to living contact with the world? We too can waft a breath of gentleness through the world by laughing at our own folly as well as that of others. "Guard yourself from despondency above all," said the Seer of Lublin, "for it is worse and more harmful than sin. When the Evil Urge wakens desires in man, he is not concerned with plunging him into sin, but with plunging him into despondency by way of his sinning.[11]

It is the same with the despondency that comes to us through adversity. When one disciple complained to his teacher that it actually seems as if God were hiding his face from the unhappy being afflicted with misfortune, the rabbi replied, as we have seen: "It ceases to be a hiding, if you know it is a hiding." The Maggid of Koznitz said, "Every day, man shall go forth out of Egypt, out of distress." Sometimes this means hoping in the face of misfortune. Rabbi Yehiel Makhal of Zlotchov lived in great poverty early in life, but not for an hour did happiness desert him. When asked how he could say, day after day, "Blessed be thou . . . who has supplied my every want?", he replied, "My want is, most likely, poverty, and that is what I have been supplied with." Yehiel Mikhal said to his sons: "My life was blessed in that I never needed anything until I had it."[12] This is a staggering statement for us—a society of consumers whose "needs" are constantly being multiplied by advertising and by our own fantasies!

Hope is not the opposite of facing death. True hope is possible only *after* one faces death and goes through it—all the little deaths in life and the great death that awaits us. When some disciples of Rabbi Nahum of Tchernobil came to him weeping and complained that they had fallen prey to darkness and depression and could not lift up their heads, he said to them:

> My dear sons, do not be distressed at this seeming death which has come upon you. For everything that is in the world, is also in man. And just as on New Year's Day life ceases on all the stars and they sink into a deep sleep, in which they are strengthened, and from which they awake with a new power of shining, so those men who truly desire to come close to God, must pass through the state of cessation of spiritual life, and 'the falling is for the sake of the rising.'[13]

One must shine with one's own light and not just rely on one's studies or the light of others. To do this we must pray not just for the petty needs of the hour but for our redemption. We must ask of life much, rather than little. That does not mean that we should spend our time brooding over what we are getting out of life. On the contrary, only when we forget ourselves and think about the world will we begin to receive from life and, what is the same thing, find life ready to receive what we have to give.

The Tales of the Hasidim speak to my condition and, I suspect, that of many others, not only because but also *despite* the fact that they are religious. Not that I am personally "turned off" by their religious vocabulary. Yet to me it is essential to witness that all that has been said above holds as much for what I have called the "Dialogue with the Absurd" as the dialogue with God. What is in question, to me, is not what we *believe* in, but the attitudes we bring to the great and small encounters of our lives. This is the real hallowing of the everyday. The "courage to address and the courage to respond" do not depend upon a belief in God. They can exist equally well in a Doctor Rieux, the atheist healer in Camus's novel *The Plague*. Although the never-ending struggle with the plague cannot end in victory, that is no reason for giving up the struggle. This sort of stubborn trust *in spite of all* is not incompatible with the spirit of Hasidism. As we recall, Rabbi Shlomo of Karlin once said to someone: "I have no key to open you." At this the man cried out: "Then pry me open with a nail!" From this time on, the rabbi always spoke words of warm praise about him.[14]

Our Dialogue with the Absurd implies a trust that though the absurd will never be anything but absurd, meaning may emerge from our meeting with it. This means a double posture—contending with the absurd yet trusting in the meaning that arises from this contending. To understand hope and despondency, we must understand their relationship to courage and trust. Our life is lived in a continual distancing and relating, as Martin Buber has pointed out in his *Knowledge of Man*. Hope might be seen as a leaning toward or anticipating of the relationship, despondency as bogging down in the distancing and giving up hope of overcoming it. From this standpoint, trust can be seen as the midpoint between distance and relationship, courage as the courage to live in that swinging tension without taking refuge in undue hope or collapsing into despondency. From this standpoint, too, courage and trust can be seen as creatively living with the tension between present and future, expectation and disappointment, living and dying, meaning and the absurd. Hope needs to test and retest its touchstones of reality to avoid falling into sentimentality or its first cousin despair. True hope is based on trust, not on *faith that* something will be so. It is a direction of movement rather than a demonstrable progress toward an ideal or goal. In the end, our task is to meet the present with courage and trust—ready to address and ready to respond.

> Strength beyond hope and despair,
> Climbing the third stair.

Notes

Key: TH:EM = Martin Buber, TALES OF THE HASIDIM:
  THE EARLY MASTERS
  TH:LM = Buber, TALES OF THE HASIDIM: THE
  LATER MASTERS

PREFACE

1. Martin Buber, *Tales of the Hasidim: The Early Masters,* trans. by
   Olga Marx (New York: Schocken Books, 1961), "True Sorrow and
   True Joy," p. 231.
2. Maurice Friedman, *Touchstones of Reality: Existential Trust and
   the Community of Peace* (New York: E. P. Dutton, 1972), p. 29.

CHAPTER 1
HASIDISM

1. Martin Buber, *The Legend of the Baal-Shem,* trans. by Maurice
   Friedman (New York: Schocken Books, paperback, 1969), p. 49 f.
2. *Doctor Zhivago,* trans. by Max Hayward & Manya Harari (London:
   Collins and Harvill Press, 1958), p. 117.
3. TH:EM, Introduction, p. 11.

CHAPTER 2
TO TELL A STORY

1. Paul Arthur Schilpp and Maurice Friedman, Eds., *The Philosophy
   of Martin Buber* volume of *The Library of Living Philosophers*

(LaSalle, Illinois: 1967), Walter Kaufmann, "Buber's Religious Significance," p. 680.

2. Martin Buber, *Hasidism and Modern Man*, Ed. & trans. with an Introduction by Maurice Friedman (New York: Horizon Books, 1973), p. 26.

3. Gershom G. Scholem, *Major Trends in Jewish Mysticism* (New York: Schocken Books, 1961), p. 349.

4. TH:EM, Preface, p. v f.

5. Martin Buber, *Tales of the Hasidim: The Later Masters,* trans. by Olga Marx (New York: Schocken Books, 1961), "Generations," p. 92 f.

6. TH:LM, "And the Fire Abated," p. 103.

7. TH:LM, "In Every Generation," p. 99.

8. TH:EM, "How to Say Torah," p. 107.

Chapter 3
"Why Were You Not Zusya?"

1. Martin Buber, *Tales of the Hasidim: The Early Masters,* trans. by Olga Marx (New York: Schocken Books, paperback, 1961), p. 135—"Originality."

2. TH:EM, p. 313—"The Way."

3. TH:EM, p. 121—"The Teaching of the Soul," p. 286—"The Story of the Cape."

4. TH:EM, p. 228 f.—"Perhaps."

Chapter 4
Serving God with the "Evil" Urge

1. TH:EM, p. 66.

2. Martin Buber, *The Origin and Meaning of Hasidism,* ed. & trans. with an Introduction by Maurice Friedman (New York: Horizon Books, 1960), p. 65f.

3. *Ibid.,* p. 77.

4. Buber, *Hasidism and Modern Man,* p. 142.

5. Martin Buber, *Ten Rungs: Hasidic Sayings,* trans. by Olga Marx (New York: Schocken Books, 1947), p. 37 f.—"In the Dust"; TH:EM, p. 66—"The Limits of Advice"; Buber, *The Origin and Meaning of Hasidism,* p. 166 f.; TH:LM, p. 17—"Everywhere."

6. Buber, *Ten Rungs,* p. 40—"On the Earth"; TH:EM, p. 269—"What He Prayed With."
7. Buber, *The Origin and Meaning of Hasidism,* p. 181.
8. Buber, *Ten Rungs,* pp. 49, 71. Cf. TH:EM, p. 191—"Be Holy."
9. Buber, *Hasidism and Modern Man,* p. 188.
10. Buber, *Hasidism and Modern Man,* pp. 196 f., 292 f.
11. Buber, *The Origin and Meaning of Hasidism,* p. 166.
12. TH:EM, p. 82—"After the Death of His Wife."
13. TH:EM, p. 187 f.—"Sleep"; TH:LM, p. 225—"What He Learned in Lublin," p. 302—"The Honest Sleep."
14. TH:EM, p. 226—"In a Hurry."
15. TH:EM, p. 145 f.—"Multiply"; TH:LM, p. 51—"With the Same Passion," p. 59—"The Nature of Service," p. 241 f.—"In a Brothel."
16. TH:EM, p. 122—"Sefirot," p. 135—"All Joys," p. 145—"Man and the Evil Urge."
17. TH:EM, p. 161—"Gamblers," p. 219—"Envy."
18. TH:EM, p. 315 f.—"The Merry Sinner"; TH:LM, p. 53 f.—"Two Kinds of Zaddikim."
19. TH:LM, p. 292—"The Alphabet."
20. TH:LM, p. 306 f.—"A Sermon."
21. TH:EM, p. 68 f.—"The Hose Maker."

CHAPTER 5
KAVANA

1. Buber, *Hasidism and Modern Man,* p. 189.
2. TH:LM, p. 163—"Not by Bread Alone."
3. TH:EM, p. 93 f.—"Medicine."
4. *The Philosophy of Martin Buber,* Martin Buber, "Replies to My Critics," trans. by Maurice Friedman, IX. "On Hasidim," pp. 732–739. Cf. Maurice Friedman, *Martin Buber's Life and Work: The Later Years—1945–1965* (New York: E. P. Dutton, 1984), Chap. 12—"The Interpretation of Hasidism: Buber versus Scholem," pp. 286–288, 293 f.
5. TH:EM, p. 64—"The Axe."
6. TH:LM, p. 166—"The Original Meaning."
7. TH:EM, p. 13 f., p. 49—"The Form," p. 51—"How Ahijah Taught Him."

8. TH:LM, p. 116—"Freedom of Choice," p. 170—"Everywhere," p. 276—"To What Purpose Was Man Created?", p. 277—"God's Dwelling."
9. Buber, *Hasidism and Modern Man,* p. 176.
10. Ibid., p. 42 f.
11. TH:EM, p. 88—"To Himself," p. 124—"The Place of Man," p. 198 f.—"On the Earth," "Nothing at All," p. 282—"The Worst."
12. TH:EM, p. 125 f.—"The One Thing," p. 149—"Sanctification of God"; TH:LM, p. 50 f.—"The Streets of Nehardea," p. 92—"The Way of Life."
13. TH:LM, p. 166—"Accepting the World," p. 305—"Throw Up the world," p. 317—"The Two Worlds."
14. Buber, *Hasidism and Modern Man,* p. 175.
15. TH:EM, p. 105—"Ten Principles."
16. TH:EM, p. 104—"The Strong Thief."
17. TH:EM, p. 125—"The Prayerbook"; TH:LM, p. 139—"The Loftiest Prayer."
18. TH:EM, p. 275 f.—"The Venture of Prayer"; TH:LM, p. 145—"Before Going to Pray," p. 153—"The Nature of Prayer," p. 169—"Exchange of Strength," "Into the Word."
19. TH:EM, p. 73—"The Crowded House of Prayer," p. 214 f.—"The Hoarse Reader," "Absent Ones," "Babbling Sounds."
20. TH:EM, p. 69—"The Busy Man's Prayer," p. 213—"His Wife's Prayer"; TH:LM, p. 55 f.—"The Counterruse"; TH:EM, p. 150—item #4.
21. TH:LM, p. 249—"All Bones," p. 302—"Basic Attitudes."
22. TH:LM, p. 145 f.—"The Secret Prayer."
23. TH:EM, p. 97—"The Two Wicks," p. 69 f.—"The Little Whistle," p. 180—"The Air of That Land," p. 210 f.—"An Interruption."
24. TH:EM, p. 235—"The Blessings," p. 246—"Zusya's Devotions," p. 211—"The Wish."

Chapter 6
Overcoming Dualism

1. TH:EM, p. 174—"The Rope Dancer."
2. Buber, *Hasidism and Modern Man,* pp. 38–40.
3. TH:EM, p. 132, middle paragraph—"For Truth."
4. TH:EM, p. 269—"What He Prayed With."
5. TH:LM, p. 61—"Penance."

CHAPTER 7
TEACHING AND LEARNING

1. TH:EM, p. ix f.
2. TH:EM, p. 5.
3. TH:EM, p. 8.
4. Martin Buber, *Ten Rungs: Hasidic Sayings,* trans. by Olga Marx (New York: Schocken Books, 1962), "Giving and Receiving," p. 60, "Upon Thy Heart," p. 64.
5. TH:EM, p. 18.
6. TH:EM, p. 52—"Knowledge," p. 95 f.—"Forgetting," p. 99 f.— "Reception," p. 287—"Knowledge."
7. TH:EM, p. 131 f.—"For Truth," p. 236 f.—"The Word."
8. TH:EM, p. 91—"How We Should Learn"; TH:LM, p. 153—"The Chain"; TH:EM, p. 163—"With the Prince of the Torah."
9. TH:EM, p. 191 f.—"Preparation," p. 268 f.—"Where Are You?"; TH:LM, p. 148 f.—"Testimony of the Disciple."
10. TH:EM, p. 51—"For You," p. 101 f.—"Palm and Cedar."
11. TH:EM, p. 200—"Conversion," p. 61—"Losing the Way."
12. TH:EM, p. 92—"The Fiftieth Gate."
13. TH:EM, p. 72—"Hospitality."
14. TH:EM, p. 106—"The Ball."
15. TH:EM, p. 316—"Alien Thoughts," "Patchwork."
16. TH:LM, p. 254—"The Obliging Dream."
17. TH:LM, p. 179 f.—"Not without the Garment of Flesh," p. 269— "From Now On," p. 271 f.—"The Offer."
18. TH:EM, p. 94—"Fine Words."
19. TH:EM, p. 104—"The Between Stage," p. 111—"At the Pond."
20. TH:EM, p. 126—"The Ear That Is No Ear"; TH:LM, p. 150—"A Pregnancy."
21. *Against Silence: The Voice and Vision of Elie Wiesel,* selected and ed. by Irving Abrahamson, Vol. III (New York: The Holocaust Library, 1985), "The Great Adventure," p. 256 f.
22. Ibid., p. 297.

CHAPTER 8
LOVE AND COMMUNITY

1. Martin Buber, *Tales of the Hasidim: The Later Masters,* trans. by Olga Marx, (New York: Schocken Books, paperback, 1961), p. 214—"Resignation."

2. TH:EM, p. 160—"The Coachman," "The Horses," p. 237 f.—
"Suffering," p. 245—"Zusya and the Birds."
3. TH:LM, p. 85—"Interruption," p. 87—"The Love of Man," p.
151 f.—"Drugs."
4. TH:LM, p. 177—"Window and Curtain," p. 150—"Men Can
Meet."
5. TH:EM, p. 53 f.
6. TH:EM, p. 54 f., p. 172 f.—"Zaddik and Hasidim"; TH:LM, p.
54—"Zaddikim and Hasidim."
7. TH:EM, p. 64 f.—"The Word of the Disciple."
8. Cf. Samuel H. Dresner, *The Zaddik* (London & New York: Abelard-
Schuman, 1960).
9. Maurice Friedman, *The Human Way: A Dialogical Approach to
Religion and Human Experience* (Chambersburg, PA: Anima Publications, 1982), p. 141.
10. Ibid., p. 150.
11. Ibid., p. 151.
12. TH:EM, p. 126.
13. TH:EM, p. 126, p. 129 f.—"More Love."
14. TH:LM, p. 220—"Give and Take," p. 263 f.—"Covenant with the
Philistines," and see again p. 283—"Comparing One to Another."
15. TH:EM, p. 126 f.—"Differences," p. 137—"Testimony," p. 150—
2nd item, p. 152—"Participation."
16. TH:LM, p. 213—"Looking for the Way."
17. TH:LM, p. 191 f.—"The Offering."
18. TH:EM, p. 151—"The Rich Man."
19. TH:EM, p. 191—"Poor Man and Rich Man," p. 292—"Rich People's Food"; TH:LM, p. 197—"The Other Half."
20. TH:EM, p. 159—"The Servant," p. 225—"Drudgery."
21. TH:EM, p. 161—"The Thieves," p. 163—"What Does It Matter?"
22. TH:EM, p. 190 f.—"The Ring"; TH:LM, p. 242—"Charity."
23. TH:EM, p. 289—"A Prayer," p. 156—"Love for Enemies," p.
159—"The Radish Eater," p. 161—"Renegades."
24. TH:EM, p. 189 f.—"The Enemy."
25. TH:LM, p. 267—"The Good Enemy," p. 283 f.—"The False
Peace," p. 264—"World Peace and Soul Peace."

CHAPTER 9
HEALING AND HELPING

1. TH:EM, p. 277.
2. TH:LM, p. 257 f.—"Young Trees."

3. TH:EM, p. 242 f.—"The Bold-faced and the Shame-faced."
4. TH:EM, p. 71—"To One Who Admonished," p. 142 f.—"Heavy Penance."
5. Buber, *The Origin and Meaning of Hasidism,* p. 142f.
6. TH:EM, p. 60 f.—"The Passage of Reproof."
7. TH:EM, p. 121—"The Breaking of the Vessels," p. 241—"Zusya and the Sinner," p. 241 f.—"Joint Penance."
8. TH:EM, p. 244 f.—"Zusya and His Wife."
9. TH:LM, p. 217 f.—"Not Yet!"; TH:EM, p. 278—"Showing and Concealing."
10. TH:EM, p. 102—"Nearness."
11. TH:EM, p. 109 f.—"The List of Sins."
12. TH:EM, p. 196—"The Letter."
13. TH:EM, p. 255 f.—"The Penitent."
14. TH:EM, p. 256 f.—"The Impure Fire."
15. Buber, *Hasidism and Modern Man,* p. 86.
16. TH:EM, p. 277 f.—"The Cure."
17. TH:EM, p. 290—"For His Sick Son," p. 307—"Purification of Souls"; TH:LM, p. 90—"The Dance of Healing."
18. TH:LM, p. 96 f.—"The Right Kind of Help."
19. TH:EM, p. 164—"The Standard"; TH:LM, p. 243—"Decision."
20. TH:EM, p. 142—"Through the Hat."
21. Maurice Friedman, *The Healing Dialogue in Psychotherapy* (New York: Jason Aronson, Inc., 1985), Chap. 17—"Empathy, Identification, Inclusion, Intuition," p. 203.
22. TH:EM, p. 128—"Concerning Anger."
23. TH:EM, p. 244—"Get Thee Out of Thy Country."
24. TH:EM, p. 277—"To Open."
25. TH:LM, p. 102—"Enduring Pain."

CHAPTER 10
THE LIMITS OF HELPING

1. TH:EM, p. 48—"Themselves"; TH:LM, p. 126—"Refusal," p. 165—"The Flame Goes Out," p. 168—"He Called to Them," p. 193—"The Morning Prayer."
2. TH:EM, p. 71—"Truth," p. 315—"Wicked and Righteous."
3. TH:LM, p. 230—"Holy Despair."
4. TH:EM, p. 34—Introduction, p. 42—"Obstacles to Blessing."
5. TH:EM, p. 53—"The Deaf Man."
6. TH:EM, p. 66—"Writing Down."
7. TH:EM, p. 67—"The Sermon."

8. TH:EM, p. 133—"Barrier," p. 305 f.—"What Ten Hasidim Can Accomplish," p. 308—"The Obstacle," p. 316—"Alien Thoughts."
9. TH:LM, p. 111—"Turning Point."
10. TH:LM, p. 19.
11. TH:LM, p. 167—"For the Sake of Others."
12. TH:LM, p. 248—"All and Each."
13. TH:EM, p. 308—"Lighter"; TH:LM, p. 151—"The Suffering He Took Over."
14. TH:LM, p. 288 f.—"The Sacred Goat."

CHAPTER 11
DIALOGUE AND TRUST

1. TH:LM, p. 170—"Everywhere."
2. TH:LM, p. 70—"Of Modern Inventions."
3. Martin Buber, *The Tales of Rabbi Nachman*, trans. by Maurice Friedman (New York: Horizon Books, 1969; Avon Books—Discussion Books, 1970), p. 36.
4. Ibid., p. 40.
5. TH:LM, p. 145—"The Secret Prayer."
6. TH:LM, p. 66 f.
7. TH:LM, p. 57.

CHAPTER 12
GOD IS PRAYER

1. Abraham Joshua Heschel, *Man's Quest for God: Studies in Prayer and Symbolism* (New York: Charles Scribner's Sons, 1954), p. 15 f.
2. Martin Buber, *Eclipse of God: Studies in the Relation Between Religion and Philosophy* (New York: Harper & Row, Harper Torchbooks, 1957), "God and the Spirit of Man," trans. by Maurice Friedman, pp. 126, 129.
3. Buber, *Ten Rungs,* p. 30—"Disturbance from Within."
4. Ibid., "The Right Kind of Altar."
5. TH:EM, p. 74—"One Small Hand"; Silvio Fittipaldi, O.S.A., *How to Pray Always Without Always Praying* (Notre Dame, Indiana: Fides/Claretian, paperback, 1978).
6. Heschel, *Man's Quest for God,* pp. 64–66.
7. TH:EM, Buber's Introduction, p. 30, p. 49 f.—"Trembling."

8. TH:EM, p. 60—"The Battle Against Amalek," p. 65—"Praying in the Field."
9. TH:EM, p. 70—"The Court Sweeper."
10. TH:EM, p. 253—"His Watch"; TH:LM, p. 154—"The Hole in the Lung," p. 167—"Self-Conquest."
11. TH:EM, p. 97—"Two Wicks."
12. TH:EM, p. 124—"The Easy Death."
13. TH:LM, p. 199—"The Perfect Swimmer."
14. TH:EM, p. 97—"Hide and Seek," p. 125—"He Is Your Psalm," p. 185 f.—"The Messiah and Those Who Pray," "The Tears of Esau."
15. TH:LM, p. 194—"The Foolish Request."
16. TH:EM, p. 289—"Testimony," p. 317 f.—"The Harpist"; TH:LM, p. 140 f.—"The Renewed Soul."
17. Buber, *Ten Rungs,* p. 30, "God Sings."
18. TH:LM, p. 158—"I Believe," p. 169—"The One Who Knows Not How to Ask," p. 205—"God's Prayer," p. 280—"Worry."
19. TH:LM, p. 304—"Like the Ox."
20. TH:EM, p. 246 f.—"Fear of God."

CHAPTER 13
THE WORLD OF DEATH

1. TH:EM, p. 284 f.—"The Rope That Gave."
2. TH:LM, p. 120—"The Table," p. 269—"The Craving," p. 302—"A Beautiful Death"; TH:EM, p. 83 f.—"Of the Baal Shem's Death"; TH:LM, p. 250—"Two Doors"; Louis I. Newman, *The Hasidic Anthology: Tales and Teachings of the Hasidim* (New York: Schocken Books, paperback, 1963), p. 71, #13.
3. TH:EM, p. 249—"Zusya, and Fire and Earth"; Newman, *Hasidic Anthology,* p. 72, #16, p. 441, #4, p. 267, #16.
4. TH:LM, p. 195—"Conflagration"; Newman, *Hasidic Anthology* p. 351, #1.
5. TH:EM, p. 271—"Seeing," p. 136—"Mourning."
6. TH:EM, p. 231—"The Dance"; TH:LM, p. 137—"The Ultimate Joy."
7. TH:EM, p. 136—"The Parting"; TH:LM, p. 197—"Do Not Stop!"
8. TH:LM, p. 171—"Not to Fear Death"; Newman, *Hasidic Anthology,* p. 200, #1; TH:LM, p. 250—"The Scarf," p. 252—"To Clutch at Life," p. 259—"For the Sake of Redemption.
9. TH:LM, p. 311—"In the Dust," "The Heart Remains."

10. TH:LM, p. 268—"The Meaning"; TH:EM, p. 83 f.—"Of the Baal Shem's Death."
11. TH:LM, p. 271—"Dying and Living."

CHAPTER 14
HOPE AND DESPONDENCY

1. Maurice Friedman, *Touchstones of Reality,* Chap. 17—"Existential Trust: The Courage to Address and the Courage to Respond."
2. TH:EM, p. 123—"On the Day of Destruction."
3. TH:LM, p. 173—"Most Important."
4. TH:EM, p. 231—"True Sorrow and True Joy."
5. TH:EM, p. 282—"The Worst"; TH:LM, p. 257—"The Great Crime"; TH:EM, p. 315 f.—"The Merry Sinner"; TH:LM, p. 95—"His Heart."
6. TH:LM, p. 305—"Throw Up the World," p. 308—"The Three Questions."
7. TH:EM, p. 308—"Lighter"; TH:LM, p. 68—"the Two Caps."
8. TH:LM, p. 315—"The Real Exile"; TH:EM, p. 267—"Concerning Ardent Zeal."
9. TH:LM, p. 262—"True and False Turning."
10. TH:LM, p. 117—"Like a Vessel," p. 318—"On Growing Old"; Buber, *Eclipse of God,* Chap. 1—"Prelude: Report on Two Talks," trans. by Maurice Friedman, p. 6.
11. TH:EM, p. 109—"The List of Sins," p. 315—"Sin and Despondency."
12. TH:EM, p. 122—"Hiding," p. 290—"Everyday," p. 138—"The Want."
13. TH:EM, p. 173—"Words of Comfort."
14. TH:EM, p. 277—"To Open."

Index